Young Searchers

Andrew and Andrea Marple

ISBN: 978-1-78364-481-0

THE OPEN BIBLE TRUST
Fordland Mount, Upper Basildon,
Reading, RG8 8LU, UK.

www.obt.org.uk

Table of Contents

****

Publications of The Open Bible Trust must be in accordance with its evangelical, fundamental and dispensational basis. However, beyond this minimum, writers are free to express whatever beliefs they may have as their own understanding, provided that the aim in so doing is to further the object of The Open Bible Trust. A copy of the doctrinal basis is available on **www.obt.org.uk** or from:

THE OPEN BIBLE TRUST
Fordland Mount, Upper Basildon,
Reading, RG8 8LU, UK

About the authors

Andrew Marple studied at Nottingham University where he read chemical engineering. Since leaving university he has worked in the oil and gas industry. This has seen him work in Aberdeen as well as a variety of postings around the world.

Andrea Marple studied music at Sheffield University then trained as a primary school teacher. She is the eldest daughter of the late David Horobin. David was an original Trustee when the O.B.T began in 1984 and he started the *Young Searchers* articles for *Search*. Inspired to continue his work, Andrea has been helping Andrew since 2001. In recent years abroad she has enjoyed both time as a teacher and also being a housewife.

At present Andrew and Andrea live and worship near Aberdeen with their three sons.

Introduction

In August 2009, our 52nd *Young Searchers* article was published in the Open Bible Trust's bi-monthly *Search* magazine. For some time we had been requested to make a compilation of these and publish them in a book. However, we wanted to wait until we had 52, so that there would be one for each week of the year.

If Sunday Schools or schools wish to use these *Young Searchers* they are free to copy them, and there is no need to seek permission. The painting on the cover is from a limited edition print by Maree entitled *Sunday School.*

Many thanks to all the ministers, speakers, pastors, and family who have taught us over the years and provided the inspiration for the articles.

Old Testament

S	S	S	E	G	D	U	J	A	M	O	S
N	U	B	M	A	L	A	C	H	I	A	H
O	C	B	E	L	A	K	I	S	M	N	A
I	I	S	A	I	A	H	I	U	O	O	I
T	T	E	Z	S	O	S	E	N	S	J	R
A	I	B	O	J	E	L	P	L	G	O	A
T	V	M	I	N	U	M	B	E	R	S	H
N	E	H	E	M	I	A	H	O	U	H	C
E	L	G	Z	H	A	N	O	J	T	U	E
M	A	E	R	E	H	T	S	E	H	A	Z
A	C	H	A	I	N	A	H	P	E	Z	E
L	Y	M	O	N	O	R	E	T	U	E	D

AMOS
JOEL
RUTH
JOB
JONAH
KINGS
EZRA
ESTHER
SAMUEL
ISAIAH
GENESIS
JUDGES
JOSHUA

LAMENTATIONS   DEUTERONOMY   NEHEMIAH
LEVITICUS   ZECHARIAH   MALACHI
ZEPHANIAH   PSALMS   NUMBERS

Young Searchers

By Andrew and Andrea Marple

Strength

What does it mean when a person is described as having strength? It can mean that they are physically strong like a weightlifter or athlete, or mentally strong - being able to say "no" to a second helping! It can also describe someone's personality, their character or determination.

Have you heard of Samson? We can read about his life in Judges Chapters 13 to 16. Use an NIV Bible to help you to answer these questions about him:

1. Who was Samson's father? (Judges Ch.13, v.2)_____

2. Which clan or tribe was he from? (Judges Ch.13, v.2)_____

3. Verse 5 of chapter 13 is a key verse. Fill in the gaps:

"Because you will conceive and give birth to a _____. No _____ may be used on his head, because the boy is to be a _____ set apart to God from _____, and he will begin the deliverance of _____ from the hands of the _____."

4. Which animal did Samson kill with his bare hands? (Judges Ch.14, v.6)

_____.

5. What did Samson later find in the body of the animal? (Judges Ch.14, v.8) _____.

6. What did Samson use to kill a thousand Philistine men? (Judges Ch.15, v.15) _____

Samson had great strength, which at first was a secret from those around him.

7.Which part of his body does Samson need to keep in order to stay strong? (Judges Ch.16, v.17) _____.

8.Who does he tell this secret to? (Judges Ch.16, v.17) _____

9.What will Samson become if his head is shaved? (Judges Ch.16, v.17)

_____.

10.What was Samson's final act before he died? (Judges Ch.16, v.29-30)

_____

Samson's great physical strength was given to him by God, but he wasted it and didn't make the most of his opportunities. Although God was present in his life, He didn't overwhelm Samson's will, and we see the evidence of his mistakes and weaknesses.

Despite this, God chose Samson to lead Israel for twenty years, at the end of which he had completed God's mission for him to "begin the deliverance of Israel from the hands of the Philistines." (Judges Ch.13, v.5). Samson's name even appears as one of the faithful people of Israel in Hebrews chapter 11, verse 32.

God is always with us. He sees our weaknesses, missed opportunities and mistakes, but as with Samson, it is never too late for us to put our trust in Him so that He can strengthen us and use us.

> **Dear Lord,**
>
> **We thank You for Your faithfulness. Thank You that You know everything about us. Help us to realise that we don't need to be perfect to be used by You. We know You have a purpose for our lives and we pray for Your strength and guidance. In Christ's name we pray, Amen.**

Young Searchers

By Andrew and Andrea Marple

Taking the First Step

Have you recently experienced a new start or change in your life? Most school years start with a new class and teacher. Perhaps you have recently started a new job or moved house. Whether you do it alone or with others, it takes a certain amount of bravery to take that first step into the unknown.

The Old Testament book of Joshua tells us about a new beginning for a whole nation – Israel. Find this book and read the whole of chapter 3.

The Israelites had been in the desert for 40 years since escaping from the slavery of Egypt, led by Moses. They were waiting to enter the land that God had promised them. Due to their own disobedience, they had had to wait a long time, but change was coming!

Chapter 3 starts with the people of Israel sitting on the banks of the River Jordan, which is all that separated them from their new beginning. However, it was springtime and the river was at its most powerful. On the other side of the river, fierce enemies occupied the land.

The person God chose to lead His people across to the land He had promised them was Joshua. He was the next great leader after Moses. What do we know about Joshua? He was originally called Hoshea (Numbers ch.13 v.8) but then Moses in v.16 changed his name to Joshua. This means the Lord saves or gives victory. The Greek form of Joshua is Jesus.

However, it was the priests who stepped into the water first, carrying the Ark of the Covenant. The ark was Israel's most sacred treasure and a symbol of God's presence and power. As the river miraculously stopped flowing, the priests and the ark continued into the centre of the river-bed and remained there until the entire people of Israel had passed to the other side and into their promised land. So what can we learn from this Bible passage for our own lives today?

God instructed the priests to take that first step into the river whilst it was still a raging torrent. Likewise, there will be situations in all our lives where God is asking us to take the first step into seemingly difficult situations.

God was with his people in the form of the Ark of the Covenant and protected them as they all crossed to the other side. Likewise, God will be with us when he asks us to do something.

Cross out one of the two letters in each square to reveal words from Joshua chapter 3.

Dear Lord,

You are our strength and our guide. Give us courage in new situations where we are unsure and help us to remember that You are always with us. In Christ's name we pray, Amen.

     Published by The Open Bible Trust

Young Searchers

By Andrew and Andrea Marple

Zechariah

Have you ever said a prayer to God in which you made a highly improbable, or even impossible request? You wanted something so badly that, although it seemed unlikely to happen, you knew it was worth praying for? We do it because we trust from the Bible that God is "able to do immeasurably more than all we ask or imagine…" (Ephesians 3:20).

Chapter 1 of Luke tells us about Zechariah. It describes a man who was willing to ask God for His help, trusting that his prayer would be answered. It shows us how God can accomplish great things through someone who prays, believes, and obeys. Let's read verses 5-25 and 57-80 and then look at the following questions:

Who was Zechariah?

Zechariah was a Jewish priest, descended from Aaron, the first priest of Israel. He was married to Elisabeth, who was also descended from Aaron. Luke tells us that they were both quite old and had not been able to have any children, much to their regret.

What did the Jewish priests do?

A Jewish priest was the equivalent of our church ministers; they worked at the Temple in Jerusalem, looking after its upkeep and teaching the Jews about God's word. In the time of Zechariah, there were over 20,000 priests throughout Israel. They couldn't all work at the Temple at the same time, so they had been split up into 24 divisions. Each division worked for a week at a time at the Temple, before returning home.

How did Zechariah come to enter the Holy Place in the Temple?

Zechariah was a member of the Abijah division of priests and it was their turn at the Temple. One of the priests' duties was to keep the incense burning on the altar in the Holy Place. This was done twice a day: morning and evening. On this day, Zechariah was chosen to perform this duty.

Who appeared to Zechariah in the Holy Place in the Temple?

"Then an angel of the Lord appeared to him, standing at the right side of

---

Imagine that you are Zechariah on that day. Write down what all your senses would have been experiencing when you: entered the Temple; saw the angel Gabriel appear; and heard that the Messiah was coming.

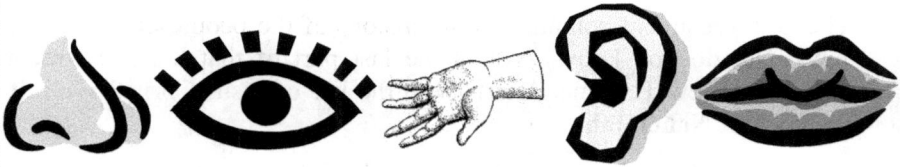

For example - the silent Temple; the smell of the incense; the beauty of the Holy Place; the words of your prayers.

---

the altar of incense." (v.11)

What did Gabriel Tell Zechariah?

Zechariah was to have a son who would bring joy, delight and rejoicing. (v.14) "...for he will be great in the sight of the Lord." (v.15). The child was to be given the name John - meaning "The Lord is gracious" - and was later known as John the Baptist. Zechariah's son was going to "...make ready a people prepared for the Lord" (v.17).

What was Zechariah's response to this wonderful news?

He didn't respond to the mention of the coming of the Messiah, but instead Zechariah expressed doubts about his own ability to father the child the angel had promised him. Having trusted enough to make the improbable request of God, he seemingly couldn't believe that his prayer had been answered, unless he had a sign. Zechariah's disbelief meant that he was struck dumb until the moment he named his new- born son (v.63-64).

We can read more about John the Baptist's life in Luke chapter 3.

What is our response to Zechariah's story?

God listens to faithful prayers. We need to believe that He is answering them in His own way, and remember that God can make things happen in seemingly impossible situations.

Young Searchers

By Andrew and Andrea Marple

A Wall of Prayers

The Old Testament contains a long history of the people of Israel – the Jews. But do you know what is the last part of that historical record before the New Testament starts with the life of Jesus Christ? Well, it's the book of **Nehemiah**.

When we are reading a passage in the Bible, it is always important to find out what had happened before the piece we are reading – to put it in **context**. To properly understand the book of Nehemiah we have to go back to 586 B.C. – that is 586 years before Jesus Christ was born. In that year, Jerusalem had been destroyed and many of the Jews had been taken captive to Babylon. By the time that Nehemiah was written (445 B.C.), there had been two groups of exiled Jews who had returned to **Jerusalem** and the **temple** there had been rebuilt.

Read the whole of the first six chapters of Nehemiah, perhaps in a translation of the Bible that makes it easier to understand if you have one. However, we can summarise these chapters as follows:

Nehemiah is still in exile in Babylon and works as "cupbearer" for **King Artaxerxes**. He hears from some Jews that the walls of Jerusalem are broken down, leaving the city, its newly rebuilt temple and its people unprotected from the nations and enemies around about.

Nehemiah is so upset and saddened by this news that he asks the king if he can return to Jerusalem and rebuild the city walls. King Artaxerxes not only agrees, but also provides Nehemiah with wood to help with the job.

Nehemiah arrives in Jerusalem and organises the Jews there to rebuild the walls. Despite problems and opposition, we read in 6:15-16:

"So the wall was completed on the twenty-fifth day of Elul, in fifty-two days. When all our enemies heard about this, all the surrounding nations were afraid because they realised that this work had been done with the help of our God."

Answer the following questions on Nehemiah:

1. What does Nehemiah do when he hears the bad news from Jerusalem (1:4-11)?

2. What does Nehemiah do before he asks for the king's permission to return to Jerusalem to rebuild the walls (2:4)?

3. What does Nehemiah do after being taunted and made fun of (4:4-5)?

4. What does Nehemiah do when he is threatened (4:9)?

The answer to all these questions is that **Nehemiah prayed**. In response to bad news; needing courage; being made fun of; and being threatened, Nehemiah's first reaction is to pray.

Today, our prayers to God are still just as powerful to help us solve problems, overcome difficulties and to find out what God wants us to do. We might not all be working on projects for God as large as rebuilding the walls of Jerusalem, but we can be sure that prayer to God can guide all our work for Him, no matter how small that seems to us.

Dear Lord,

Just as Nehemiah looked to You in prayer, help us to trust our problems, concerns and ambitions to You. Bless all our projects.

In Christ's name we pray, Amen.

Young Searchers

By Andrew and Andrea Marple

Where to draw the line?

King Nebuchadnezzar II ascended to the throne of the great empire of Babylonia, which stretched from the Persian Gulf to the Mediterranean Sea, in 605 B.C. He was feared throughout the then-known world and, in the first year of his reign, his armies had captured Jerusalem. As was their practice, they carried off to Babylon (some 500 miles away) the brightest and most promising members of the royal family and nobility. In Babylon they were to undergo three years of training and indoctrination before entering the king's service (you can read the Biblical account of this in Daniel 1:1-5).

Among the first group of people taken from Jerusalem to Babylon were Daniel and his three friends. These young people must have been very frightened; uprooted from their families and their Jewish culture, they were transported far away into a completely strange alien environment. They were even given Babylonian names as Daniel 1:6 tells us. It would have been very easy for Daniel and his friends to have given up their beliefs and principles and to have adopted the pagan practices of the Babylonians. However, they had great faith in God and a strong commitment to their Jewish principals: they knew where to draw the line.

Verses 8-16 tell us that Daniel and his friends refused to eat the food and drink that King Nebuchadnezzar had given them. This food and drink had not been prepared according to the Jewish laws that God had defined for them in the Bible. Daniel and his friends stood by their convictions and their faith in God.

       Visit www.obt.org.uk for more resources

In the remaining verses of Daniel chapter 1, we are told that God rewarded the faith of Daniel and his friends, giving them wisdom and understanding; enabling them to carry out God's plan in positions of power in the Babylonian empire.

Can you help Daniel to draw the line?

Without taking your pencil from the paper, draw four straight lines that pass through the centre of each of the nine fruits:

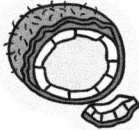

For young Christians today, our own society can seem just as alien and strange as that of Babylon in Daniel's time. We can feel pressurised into doing things that we are not comfortable with; things that are seen as 'normal' behaviour, yet we sense are wrong. We must learn from his example: whilst living in an alien culture, he knew where to draw the line, when to say "no" to what he was being asked to do and he continued to say "yes" to God's commands. Instead of direct rebellion, he negotiated with the king's official and proved to him that God's ways were best.

Dear Lord,

As we live our lives for You, we ask that You will help us to find the right words and actions in difficult situations. Be with us as we try to continue to serve and be faithful to You.

In Christ's name we pray, Amen.

Young Searchers

By Andrew and Andrea Marple

Samuel – Servant of God

Samuel is one of the few Biblical characters for who we have a complete life story: from birth, through childhood, the great works of his adult life, even retirement, and finally his death.

Samuel's Birth

1 Samuel chapter 1 tells us of Samuels' birth. His mother – Hannah – was unable to have children. So when she went to the Tabernacle, located at the religious centre of Israel – Shiloh, she prayed fervently to God. Hannah promised God that, if she was able to have a son, she would give him back to God for His service. God granted Hannah the son she so earnestly desired and he was named Samuel, which comes from the Hebrew expression for "asked of God". True to her promise, when he was old enough, Hannah placed Samuel into the hands of Eli – the priest at the Tabernacle – to be trained in the priesthood.

Samuel's Childhood

1 Samuel chapter 3 gives the familiar account of God calling Samuel to serve Him. Reread this chapter and think how you would respond if God called you to do something.

Samuel's Adult Life

Following the Exodus of the people of Israel from Egypt, God appointed a series of judges. These are not to be confused with modern judges in the law courts, but were men and women who God used to help rule and guide His people. Although each judge was different in style and approach, they all had one simple message: God will punish Israel when they disobey and turn away from Him; He will restore their power and glory when they repent and turn back to Him.

1 Samuel chapter 7 tells us that Samuel became Israel's judge at that time. He judges Israel well, saves them from the Philistine nation yet again and leads them back to God. Finally Samuel retires from his position as a judge and appoints his sons in his place.

Look at the list of judges below, as detailed in the book of Judges in the Old Testament. Look up the references, learn something about these characters and fill in their names:

Judge	Reference	Judge	Reference
O _ _ _ _ _ L	Judges 3:7-11	J _ _ R	Judges 10: 3-5
E _ _ D	Judges 3:12-30	J _ _ _ _ _ _ H	Judges 10:6-12:17
S _ _ _ _ _ R	Judges 3:31	I _ _ _ N	Judges 12: 8-10
D _ _ _ _ _ H	Judges 4 and 5	E _ _ N	Judges 12: 11,12
G _ _ _ _ N	Judges 6 to 8	A _ _ _ N	Judges 12: 13-15
T _ _ A	Judges 10: 1,2	S _ _ _ _ N	Judges 13 to 16

Samuel's Retirement

Once Samuel had retired, the people of Israel decided that they no longer want to have a judge. Instead they wanted a king like all the other nations. Although God was not pleased with this, He granted their request and it is Samuel that He again turned to and instructed him to anoint Saul as Israel's first king. Indeed it is Samuel who also anointed Israel's second king – David – when Saul constantly disobeyed God and was rejected by Him.

Samuel's Death

There is now a long period in the account of 1 Samuel until we hear of Samuel's death at the start of chapter 25: "Now Samuel died and all Israel assembled and mourned for him and they buried him at his home in Ramah".

Samuel had been Israel's most effective judge and takes his place in the "Hall of Faith" detailed in Hebrews 11 (verse 32). He shows us that we can accomplish anything in life if we have the correct relationship with God. He was a true servant of God.

Young Searchers

By Andrew and Andrea Marple

Gideon – Servant of God

In the last issue of *Young Searchers* we looked at the life of Samuel. He was one of the series of judges that God appointed following the Exodus of the people of Israel from Egypt. Each judge was different in style and approach, but they all had one simple message: God will punish Israel when they disobey and turn away from Him; He will restore their power and glory when they repent and turn back to Him. This time we will investigate the life of another judge – Gideon.

Gideon's Story

Gideon's life is set before us in the book of Judges chapters 6 to 8. Go ahead and read the whole of these three chapters.

We can see that Gideon was by no means perfect: he had weaknesses and made mistakes. Yet he truly served God and is specifically mentioned in the great Faith chapter of Hebrews 11 (verse 32) alongside all the other faithful men and women in the history of Israel.

At the start of the account of Gideon's life in Judges 6, we see that the people of Israel have yet again turned away from God and started to worship the pagan gods of the nations around them. Without God's protection they are suffering terribly at the hands of the Midianites, a nomadic people who each year plunders the crops and livestock of Israel. So impoverished and so in need became the people of Israel that they cried out to God again for salvation. As always, God heard the cries of His children and selected Gideon to serve Him and deliver His people.

The first step in the rehabilitation of Israel was for Gideon to tear down the altar that Israel had made to a god named Baal and to replace it with an altar to the Lord. Gideon carries out God's instructions but is then faced with phase 2 of the plan – the defeat and expulsion of the Midianites. At this point Gideon's faith wavers. We read in Judges 7:12 that "The Midianites, Amalekites and all the other eastern peoples has settled in the valley, thick as locusts. Their camels could no more be counted than the sand on the seashore." How could the people of Israel possibly fight all of these? God understood Gideon's lack of faith, his uncertainty and gave him a number of proofs of His power to convince him.

Miraculously, with only 300 men, Gideon utterly vanquished the Midianite armies, driving them forever from the land of Israel and securing 40 years of peace.

Can we be Gideons?

We too can do great things for God. As in the example of Gideon, we all have weaknesses and all make mistakes. Yet God will stand by us, forgive us and enable us to carry on His work. God knows that we have moments of doubt and is ready to support us and guide us at these times. We must continue to communicate through prayer with God and he will provide the resources and strength to do His work.

Gideons International

In 1899 three commercial travellers in the USA formed an association of Christian businessmen to encourage each other in their Christian faith and to spread knowledge of God through personal evangelism and united service for the Lord Jesus Christ. They chose the name *Gideons* after the Old Testament judge and leader we have been studying here. Gideon was an example of one person who, with a few chosen men, did a great work for God. Indeed the symbol of the Gideons (shown here) is a two-handled pitcher and torch, recalling Gideon's victory over the Midianites. Today, Gideons International has over 250,000 members working in 181 countries, handing out over 60 million copies of the Bible each year.

Young Searchers

By Andrew and Andrea Marple

Deborah – Servant of God

Throughout the centuries the leadership of nations has mainly rested, for better or for worse, in the hands of men. There have, however, been some notable exceptions of very strong women leaders:

Cleopatra – Pharaoh of Egypt from 69 BC to 30BC

Boudica - Queen of the Iceni tribe in England around AD 60

Queen Elizabeth I – Queen of England from 1558 to 1603

Indira Gandhi – Prime Minister of India from 1966 to 1977 and from 1980 to 1984

Golda Meir – Prime Minister of Israel from 1969 to 1974

Margaret Thatcher – Prime Minister of the UK from 1979 to 1990

Angela Merkel – Chancellor of Germany from 2005

Background

Another woman that falls into this category is Deborah. Deborah was a prophetess, the only female judge, and we can read about her life in Judges chapters 4 and 5. Chapter 4 gives us the account in prose and then chapter 5 repeats it in poetry. Go ahead and read these two chapters.

As we have seen before, the period of the judges in Israel's history was one of cycles of disobedience to God; the raising up of a judge; repentance; victory over an oppressor; and peace. Prior to Deborah, Ehud (another judge) had brought to Israel 80 years of peace. But by the time of Deborah, the people of Israel had again turned their backs on God and sinned against Him. As a result, God had allowed the Canaanites to cruelly oppress Israel for 20 long years.

Deborah's Story

Whilst holding court under a palm tree, settling the Israelites' disputes, Deborah sends for Barak. She gives him God's command to defeat Sisera and the Canaanite army. However, Barak insists that Deborah accompanies him on the attack, otherwise he won't do it. Deborah agrees, but tells Barak that, because of his doubts, the honour of killing Sisera will not be his.

With Deborah by his side, Barak does indeed defeat the army of Sisera. As prophesised, however, he does not kill Sisera himself. Instead it is Jael, another strong woman leader, who kills Sisera whilst he sleeps.

Deborah was a true servant of God, guiding Israel and providing its people with advice, good counsel and mediation. She was also called on by God to lead and direct the battle against Israel's oppressors. Deborah's life shows us that we need to be accessible to both the community around and to God if we truly want to carry out His plans for us. When we allow God into our lives and follow His commands, we can really achieve great things.

Try the challenging crossword below, the answers of which are all names of famous women from the Old Testament.

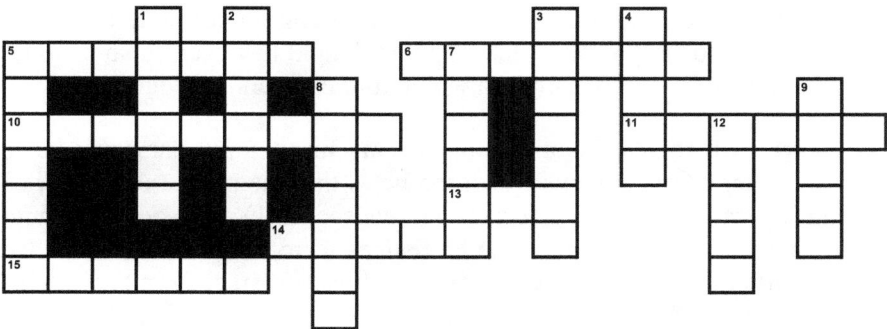

Across	Down
5. Betrayed Samson	1. Daughter of Saul and wife of David
6. Wife of Isaac	2. Mother of Joseph and Benjamin
10. First husband was Uriah	3. Queen of Israel and Ahab's wife
11. Sister of Aaron and Moses	4. Ruth's mother-in-law
13. The first woman	5. Israel's fourth judge
14. Ishmael's mother	7. Queen of Persia & Ahasuerus's wife
15. Samuel's mother	8. First husband was Nabal
	9. Wife of Abraham
	12. Mother of Boaz

Young Searchers

By Andrew and Andrea Marple

Samson – God's Power at Work

For some time now we have been looking at the judges from Israel's history. Before Israel demanded kings to rule over them, God used His judges to lead, guide and protect them. Each time that Israel turned their back on God, he sent them a judge to deliver them from their oppressors and bring them back to Him.

No series on the judges would be complete without looking at probably the most famous judge of all – Samson. Most people will have heard the "headlines" from the account of Samson given in the Bible – a man empowered by God with tremendous strength until he tells Delilah that the key to his powers is his hair. Let's look, however, in some more detail at his life, which is given a whole four chapters in Judges 13-16.

Chapter 13 recounts the miraculous events surrounding Samson's birth. The chapter starts, however, with the news that the people of Israel had again turned away from God and had consequently been delivered into the hands of the Philistines. The Philistines were a fierce people, skilled in the arts of war, who posed a constant threat to Israel from the time of Samson through to King David. An angel from God appeared to Samson's parents and told them that they were going to have a son. This angel also informed them that he was never to have his hair cut as God had special plans for him. We read in Judges 13:5 that Samson was to "… begin the deliverance of Israel from the hands of the Philistines."

Chapter 14 tells of Samson's marriage. Not for the last time, he is persuaded to reveal a secret but lives to regret it. The next time you see a tin of Lyle's Golden Syrup, have a look at the picture and the inscription beneath it and see how it relates to this Biblical account.

We learn that Samson led Israel for 20 years, protecting them from the Philistines through the use of his tremendous God-given strength. In chapter 16 we come to the most famous part of this account. The rulers of the Philistines use Delilah to trick Samson into revealing the secret to his strength. Whilst he is sleeping his hair is cut off and he is carried off in chains. Finally, Samson fulfils his mission from God to begin the deliverance of Israel from the Philistines. As his hair grows back, his powers return and he is able to bring down the great temple of the Philistines, killing himself along with thousands of Philistines.

So what can we learn from the life of Samson? Reading through Judges 13-16 we note the many wicked deeds that Samson committed, his failures and his weaknesses. However, Samson's name can still be found amongst the faithful men and women of Israel that are recorded in Hebrews chapter 11 (verse 32). To some extent Samson wasted his life and abused his God-given powers. But at the end of his life he fulfilled his mission and laid down his life for the deliverance of others.

We all make mistakes; we all sin and disappoint God. This does not mean, however, that we cannot serve God and it is never too late to hear His message and commit our lives to Him.

We thank you Lord that you can use us to do your work even though we so often fail and disappoint you. We pray that we might commit our lives to you and that you might give us the strength and powers to do great things for you.

We ask these things in Christ's name. Amen.

          Published by The Open Bible Trust

New Testament

C	O	L	O	S	S	I	A	N	S	W	E
O	Z	U	D	E	T	P	E	R	T	E	P
R	E	V	A	L	A	T	I	O	N	H	H
I	N	N	E	I	C	E	K	M	I	T	I
N	J	H	R	P	E	T	E	R	I	T	L
T	I	M	O	T	H	Y	T	C	A	A	I
H	H	E	M	J	U	E	D	A	N	M	P
I	N	E	A	U	O	L	S	T	C	A	P
A	H	M	N	D	S	U	T	I	T	E	I
N	E	T	S	E	A	K	T	S	A	P	A
S	A	P	H	I	L	E	M	O	N	N	N
M	A	R	G	A	L	A	T	I	A	N	S

TIMOTHY
PETER
JOHN
JAMES
TITUS
MARK
LUKE
ROMANS
ACTS
JUDE
PHILEMON
MATTHEW

CORINTHIANS   EPHESIANS   COLOSSIANS
PHILIPPIANS   REVELATION   GALATIANS

       Published by The Open Bible Trust

Young Searchers

By Andrew and Andrea Marple

Is that email for me?

If the Apostle Paul were alive today, he would probably be writing and sending emails rather than letters. He would be sending his *Email to the Colossians* and his *Second Email to Timothy*.

When you write an email, there are usually two main options when it comes to deciding who to send it to:

To: This is the primary audience for the message contained in the email. These people are expected to reply or act upon the message.

CC: These are the people who are not the primary destination. They would also be interested in the contents of the email, but not expected to reply or act upon the message.

So it's important when we receive an email to check whether we are the person to whom the message is being directed (To:) or if we are simply being sent something for our information (cc:).

There is an extremely important lesson here for us, which should always be directly applied as we read the Bible. When we read a passage of Scripture we should always first find out whether the message is for our reply and action, or simply for our information so that we know what is going on.

The Bible itself talks about this process, which we call **Right Division**. The following quotation is from the King James Version – 2 Tim 2:15 –

"Study to shew thyself approved unto God, a workman that needeth not to be ashamed, <u>rightly dividing the word of truth</u>."

If we rightly divide the Bible, we will recognise that much of it was written about, and for, the people of Israel. For those of us who are not the people of Israel, i.e. Gentiles, we can of course read and learn much from the whole of the Bible. Indeed as 2 Tim 3:16-17 tells us:

"All Scripture is God-breathed and is useful for teaching, rebuking, correcting and training in righteousness, so that the man of God may be thoroughly equipped for every good work."

However, there are a limited number of parts of Scripture which speak directly to us with instructions which are to govern our Christian life and witness.

For example, in Old Testament times God told the Israelites that for forgiveness of sins they must bring a sacrifice to atone for (or cover) their sin (Exodus 30:1-10). But as Christians today, we do not take that instruction for ourselves.

We believe that the sacrifice of the Lord Jesus Christ on the Cross of Calvary is the once and for all atonement for our sin. So we can learn from this Old Testament instruction but we do not need to apply it to ourselves. We rightly divide the word of truth. To go back to our email analogy, Moses would start off as follows:

To:	**The People of Israel**
cc:	The Gentiles
Subject:	**Exodus**

In the latter part of Paul's ministry, he was preaching directly to the Gentiles (see Ephesians 3:1-13). So, in the same way, Paul's letter to the Ephesians, for example, would be as follows:

To:	**The Gentiles**
cc:	The People of Israel
Subject:	**Ephesians**

Using this tool of Right Division when we read the Bible will help us to understand much better God's message to us: what He is asking us to do as we live our lives today.

Young Searchers

By Andrew and Andrea Marple

Who is my neighbour?

Do you get on well with your neighbours? Do you know each other well enough to help out in emergencies? Can you rely on them and they on you? We are of course talking about the people who live near us; but Jesus teaches us that our neighbours extend far beyond that.

Find all the places underlined in the text of the article on this map

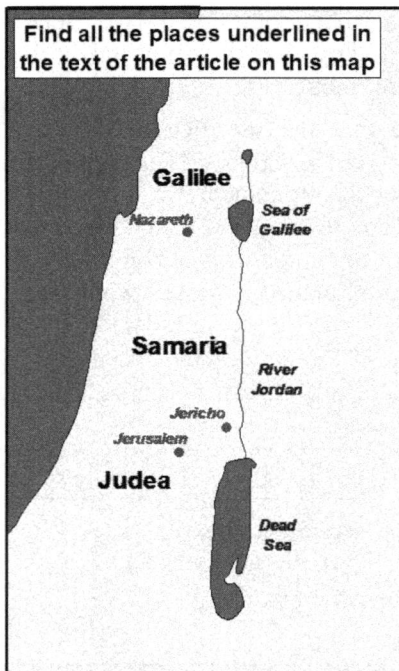

In Luke 10 v.29, Jesus was asked the very question "who is my neighbour?" by an "expert in the Law" – someone who had studied the Old Testament scriptures. In reply, Jesus tells the Parable of the Good Samaritan. Let's read Luke 10 v.30-37.

A journey from Jerusalem to Jericho

The Jewish man in the parable was travelling from Jerusalem to Jericho. This is a journey of about 17 miles, taking him down a very steep road, through a rocky desert, which was the perfect place for robbers to hide in and attack defenceless travellers.

Who were the Samaritans?

After the death of King Solomon, the kingdom of Israel broke apart into northern and southern kingdoms each with their own rulers. The Samaritans were descendents of Israelites from the northern kingdom who had intermarried with their Gentile (non-Jewish) neighbours. The Samaritans worshipped at different places and in different ways to the rest of Israel. By the time of Jesus, the Jews and the Samaritans hated each other. Jews travelling from the north to Judea in the south would normally cross over the River Jordan to the east, so that they did not have to walk through Samaria. Read Luke 9 v.51-56 to see what happened to Jesus when He made His journey from <u>Galilee</u> in the north to Jerusalem.

Attitudes to the wounded man

Try and link up the attitudes, of the characters in the Parable of the Good Samaritan, towards the wounded Jewish man by writing the following names in the boxes below – Expert in the Law, Robbers, Religious Men (Priest and Levite), Jesus Christ, Innkeeper and Samaritan:

a subject to debate and discuss

someone to use and exploit

a problem to be avoided

someone to be cared for and loved

a customer

someone worth dying for

How can we use the message of this parable today?

We can see parallels for each of the attitudes listed above in the response of the world to the recent Asian Tsunami disaster. To some people it has been something to debate and discuss; to others a problem they have tried to ignore; but, fortunately, for the vast majority of people, those affected by the disaster are human beings like ourselves to be cared for and loved.

Like the Good Samaritan, many millions of people across the world have given up time, effort and money to help. Let us hope that, like the Good Samaritan, who saw to the long-term recovery of the wounded man, this will prove to be an ongoing commitment.

          Published by The Open Bible Trust

Young Searchers

By Andrew and Andrea Marple

An "out-of-this-world" Travel Destination

If you are lucky enough to be going on a holiday this summer, chances are a fair amount of preparation has already gone into making all the necessary arrangements. Whether you've booked on-line or at a travel agent, choosing your destination is an important first step. You also have to decide how you're getting there, when you want to arrive and where you're going to stay.

In the Bible, the life of a Christian is likened to a journey. Our earthly journey is only for a comparatively short time (1 Pet 2:11-12). So where are we going after this earthly life? The Bible offers us a travel destination that is literally "out of this world"!

The Ticket – a guaranteed pledge but with one condition: "I tell you the truth, whoever hears my word *and believes him who sent me* has eternal life and will not be condemned; he has crossed over from death to life". (John 5:24).

A Seat – a privileged seat has been reserved for us: "And God raised us up with Christ and seated us with him in the heavenly realms in Christ Jesus" – Eph 2:6.

A Passport – our names must be registered with someone in authority: "Nothing impure will ever enter it, nor will anyone who does what is shameful or deceitful, but only those whose names are written in the Lamb's book of life" – Rev 21:27.

Luggage – no luggage is allowed or necessary: "For we brought nothing into the world, and we can take nothing out of it" – 1 Tim 6:7.

Immigration – we are all aliens looking for a new country: "All these people … admitted that they were aliens and strangers on earth … they were longing for a better country – a heavenly one" – Heb 11:13-16.

Injections – diseases are not known here so none are necessary: "… There will be no more death or mourning of crying or pain, for the old order of things has passed away." Rev 21:4.

Accommodation – the best rooms are already booked: "In my father's house are many rooms; if it were not so, I would have told you. I am going there to prepare a place for you." John 14:2.

The Cost – enormous and beyond our budget. Thankfully someone has already paid: "For God so loved the world that he gave his one and only Son, that whoever believes in him shall not perish but have eternal life." John 3:16.

Destination – where is this marvellous destination that's out of this world? "But our citizenship is in heaven. And we eagerly await a Saviour from there, the Lord Jesus Christ." Phi 3:20.

Have you booked to this destination of a lifetime? Can you afford to miss this fabulous offer – make a decision now!

St.Paul was famous for his Biblical journeys. Follow the route of his first missionary journey so you find all the places below and have no letters left?

Derbe
Pisidian Antioch
Cyprus
Lystra
Iconium

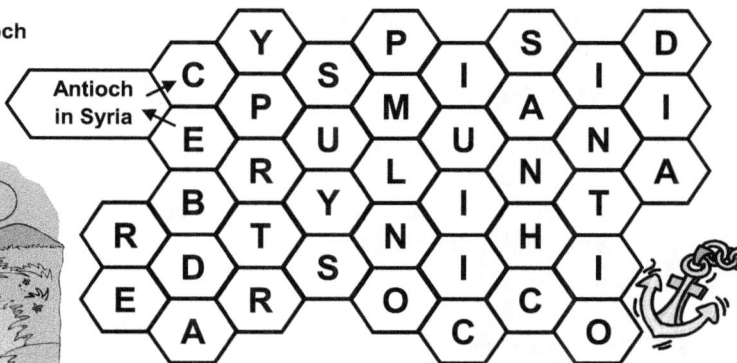

Antioch in Syria

We thank you God for the opportunity to travel to beautiful holiday destinations. Help us also as we make our way to the heavenly destination you have prepared for us. In Christ's name we pray, Amen.

Young Searchers

By Andrew and Andrea Marple

Onesimus – a Story of Reconciliation

One dictionary definition of *reconciliation* is as follows: "The act of re-establishing friendly relations between two people".

In the Bible, the letter to Philemon paints a wonderful picture of reconciliation in just 25 verses. The letter was written by Paul and details his attempt to reconcile Philemon with Onesimus. Read the book of Philemon and then answer the following questions:

1. **Who wrote this letter?** (verse 1).

2. **Who was the letter written to?** (verses 1-2).

3. **What was the relationship between Onesimus and Philemon?** (verse 16)

4. **What does the name *Onesimus* mean?** (verse 11)

As we read the letter to Philemon, we learn that Onesimus had run far away from his master, after apparently stealing from him. He had fled to Rome, but here had met the apostle Paul, become a Christian and started to work with Paul in his ministry.

Paul explains all of this to Philemon and asks him to take Onesimus back and be reconciled with him. Paul also offers to pay back any debt that Onesimus had to Philemon.

In the same way, Jesus Christ has enabled each and every one of us to be reconciled to God. Where once we were so far away, Jesus has brought us close and paid our debt of sin to God, through his death on the cross at Calvary. We are sure that God will welcome us back, no matter what we have done in the past.

Try and fill the eleven people mentioned in the letter to Philemon into the grid below:

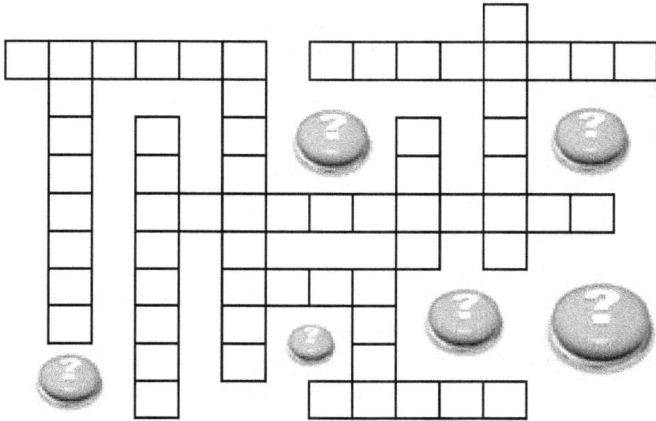

Onesimus
Philemon
Apphia
Timothy
Epaphras
Mark
Aristarchus
Demas
Luke
Archippus
Paul

As Jesus Christ did for us with God, so Paul did for Onesimus with Philemon. We too, in our daily lives, have opportunities to reconcile people. All too often barriers are thrown up between people due to disagreements and conflict; due to race and social position; due to personality and character differences. From the inspiration of Jesus Christ and Paul, we should also seek to reconcile people together and re-establish friendly relations. We should help people to set aside their differences and concentrate on those things which unite.

Dear Lord,

We thank You for Your Son, our Lord and Saviour Jesus Christ, who through His death on the cross, has reconciled us to You. We ask that You will help us in our daily lives to recah out to those who need reconcilaition. In Christ's name we pray, Amen.

Young Searchers

By Andrew and Andrea Marple

Reaching Out

The Gospels of the New Testament include numerous accounts of events from the life of Jesus Christ on Earth. Some accounts are repeated in all four Gospels, others in two or three, and some in just one Gospel.

One of the accounts that are found only in the Gospel of Luke is that of Jesus' encounter with Zacchaeus the Tax Collector. Read this account in Luke 19:1-10.

Tax Collectors

Even today if we were to rank the professions that were most disliked by society in general, the people who collect taxes on behalf of the government would certainly be very near the top of that list. However, in the time of Jesus in Israel, Tax Collectors were genuinely despised and hated by their fellow Jews.

Tax Collectors worked on behalf of the occupying Roman forces, imposing high levels of taxes that went to support the Roman Empire and all its excesses. Tax collectors were also well known for overcharging the Jewish population and keeping the extra for themselves. Any Jew who took such a job was considered to be a traitor and was virtually cast out of society.

Zacchaeus

In the first three verses of Luke 19, we are told that Zacchaeus lives in Jericho; is a leading Jew within the Roman tax-collecting business; is a very rich man; and is a short man. Indeed, he is so short that he has to climb up a sycamore-fig tree to catch a glimpse of Jesus, who was passing through Jericho.

Jesus Reaches out to Zacchaeus

Jesus immediately calls Zacchaeus by his name as he passes by the tree. He proceeds to invite himself to Zacchaeus's home, much to the displeasure of the other Jews who consider Zacchaeus unworthy of such an honour.

This encounter with Jesus has an immediate and life-changing effect on Zacchaeus. When Jesus reaches out to him, the unpopular tax collector responds to the gesture and returns the kindness; making a remarkable decision to give half his wealth to the poor and to repay anyone he has cheated four-fold.

How can we apply this today?

In our society today there are many groups of people to whom we feel we can't relate to personally – people with differing religious beliefs, moral values, sexual orientation, racial stereotypes, etc.

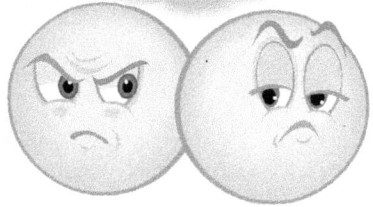

Whatever we think of how someone else lives their life, we must remember that it's not our place to judge. We are *all* sinners yet God *loves us all*.

How can we share God's love if we can't see beyond the things that divide us?

It sometimes takes courage to connect with people of differing and unfamiliar values. It's much easier to keep them at arm's length or judge their practices. But in order to respond to Christian love, people need to experience it.

> **We ask You Lord to give us the courage to reach out to *all* the people you bring into our lives. Help us not to judge but to show Your love through kindness and compassion. In Christ's name we pray. Amen.**

Visit www.obt.org.uk for more resources

In the Bible

P	E	H	C	U	E	T	A	T	N	E	P
R	W	I	Y	C	E	H	P	O	R	P	P
E	N	S	P	E	H	N	T	O	V	I	O
V	H	T	R	O	J	A	M	W	E	R	L
E	E	O	K	O	O	B	P	N	R	W	D
L	B	R	T	N	E	M	A	T	S	E	T
T	R	Y	S	R	O	N	I	M	E	N	A
S	E	N	W	I	S	D	O	M	O	R	D
I	W	O	L	G	O	S	P	E	L	A	W
P	O	E	T	R	Y	N	G	R	E	E	K
E	N	O	I	T	A	L	S	N	A	R	T
L	Y	M	A	N	A	R	E	T	A	E	D

OLD
NEW
VERSE
BOOK
HEBREW
GREEK
EPISTLE
GOSPEL
POETRY
LAW
MAJOR
MINOR

TESTAMENT   CHAPTER   VERSION
TRANSLATION   PROPHECY   WISDOM
PENTATEUCH   HISTORY

     Published by The Open Bible Trust

Young Searchers

By Andrew and Andrea Marple

Colours

Have you ever been in a church or cathedral and marvelled at the light shining through a stained glass window? The beautiful colours of the glass are used to bring to life the characters of the Bible. The various writers of the Bible used colours too, to help us better understand and imagine events that they describe. Look up the following Bible quotes and fill in the missing colours:

1. In Matthew ch.16 v.3, the Lord Jesus speaks about watching the skies for a clue on the weather. Good weather can be expected when the evening sky is _____.

2. In this very well-known quotation from Psalm ch.23 v.2, the Lord makes us lie down in _____ pastures.

3. In Mark ch.15 v.7, the soldiers mock the Lord Jesus and make him wear a _____ robe.

4. Nebuchadnezzar sets up a _____ image in Daniel ch.3 v.7 and commands everyone to worship it.

5. To save her family in Joshua ch.2 v.18, Rahab hangs a _____ cord from her window.

6. The clothes of the Lord Jesus became _____ at the transfiguration on the mountain in Matthew ch.17 v.2.

7. Acts ch.16 v.14 tells us of Lydia, a dealer in _____ cloth.

8. In Genesis ch.1 v.30, God gives animals every _____ plant to eat.

9. God told Moses and Aaron to cover a table with a _____ cloth in Numbers ch.4 v.7.

10. 1 Kings ch.18 v.45 tells us that the sky grew _____ as Ahab rode off to Jezreel.

Surely one of the most powerful images of colour is given in Isaiah ch.1 v.18, which looks towards the sacrifice that the Lord Jesus will make to pay for our sins:

"Though your sins are like *scarlet*, they shall be as *white* as snow; though they are *red* as crimson, they shall be like wool".

There is nothing that is whiter than snow, so the comparison with the red and scarlet of our sins emphasises just how much we have been cleansed by that sacrifice.

Thank you Lord for the beautiful colours in your creation and the gift of sight to enjoy them.
Help us to remember the sacrifice that Your Son made on the cross when he bleached white the scarlet and red of our sins. In Christ's name we pray, Amen.

Young Searchers

By Andrew and Andrea Marple

Trees in the Bible

In the Northern hemisphere it's summer and our trees are at their most grand and impressive; weighed down with a huge coat of vibrant green leaves. There are few more impressive sights in nature than a tall, mature tree gently moving in the wind on a glorious summer's day.

The Bible too appreciates the many qualities of trees and uses them throughout scripture. The very first reference of course goes back to Creation itself in Genesis 1:11-12:

*"Then God said, "Let the land produce vegetation: seed-bearing plants and **trees** on the land that bear fruit with seed in it, according to their various kinds." And it was so. The land produced vegetation: plants bearing seed according to their kinds and **trees** bearing fruit with seed in it according to their kinds. And God saw that it was good."*

As in the world today, in the Bible trees serve many practical purposes:

Trees for Food – Deuteronomy 20:19-20

God warns the people of Israel not to cut down fruit trees, instead they're to use other trees for building equipment, when laying siege to a city.

Trees for Shade – Genesis 18:4

Abraham advises three visitors to rest under a tree.

Trees for Fuel - Isaiah 44:14-15

Isaiah mentions a number of different types of trees and how they can be used to make a fire to bake bread on or keep warm in front of.

Trees for Building – Nehemiah 2:8

Nehemiah asks permission from King Artaxerxes to take timber from the king's forests to help rebuild the walls of Jerusalem.

Trees for Burials – Genesis 35:8

We are told that Deborah, who was nursemaid to Rebekah (Isaac's wife), was buried beneath an oak tree.

Did you know that there are over twenty-five different types of tree mentioned in the Bible? Look up the following Old Testament references from the NIV version and complete the crossword (be careful, as some references contain the names of several trees):

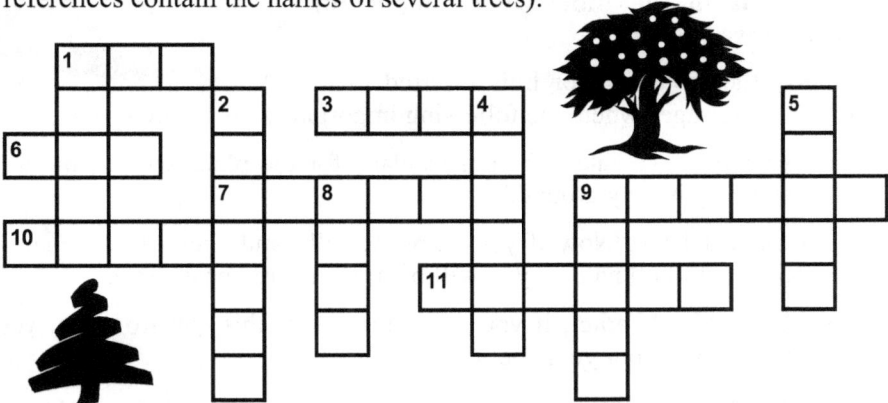

Across
1. Isaiah 1:30
3. Exodus 15:27
6. Deuteronomy 8:8
7. Hosea 4:13
9. 2 Samuel 5:23-24
10. 1 Kings 10:27
11. Jeremiah 1:11

Down
1. Judges 9:9
2. Isaiah 44:14
4. Isaiah 41:19
5. Ezekiel 31:8
8. 1 Kings 5:10
9. 1 Kings 19:4-5

Dear Lord,

We thank and praise you for the magnificence of Your nature that surrounds us, especially the trees. Help us to live our lives as trees that bear good fruit for you … In Christ's name we pray, Amen.

Young Searchers

By Andrew and Andrea Marple

A Mountain of Puzzles

Where we live in Calgary, Canada, the Rocky Mountains provide a beautiful backdrop to our daily lives. Inspired by this, what better way to start the year than with a "Mountain of Puzzles":

Mountains in the Bible where important words were spoken:

Identify the mountains or hills referred to in the Bible passages where the following important words were spoken:

1. Exodus 3 – "Take off your sandals, for the place where you are standing is holy ground".

2. Exodus 19 – "Now if you obey me fully and keep my covenant, then out of all nations you will be my treasured possession".

3. Luke 22 – "Father, if you are willing, take this cup from me; yet not my will, but yours be done".

Mountains in the Bible where important historical events took place:

Identify the mountains or hills referred to in the Bible passages where the following important historical events took place:

1. Genesis 8 – the mountain where Noah's Ark came to rest.

2. Deuteronomy 3 – a boundary of the Amorite land, which the Israelites took.

3. Deuteronomy 3 – where Moses looked at the Promised Land from afar.

4. Numbers 20 – where Aaron died.

5. 1 Kings 18 – where Elijah summoned people from all over Israel to meet him.

6. 1 Samuel 3 – Saul committed suicide here.

Hills and Mountains in the Bible:

Identify the hills or mountains referred to in the following Bible passages and then fit them all in the grid below:

Hills (across)	Mountains (down)
Jeremiah 31:39.	Psalm 42:6
1 Samuel 23:19	Judges 9:48
2 Samuel 2:24	Joshua 11:17
Judges 7:1	Judges 1:35
Nehemiah 11:21	Deuteronomy 32:49

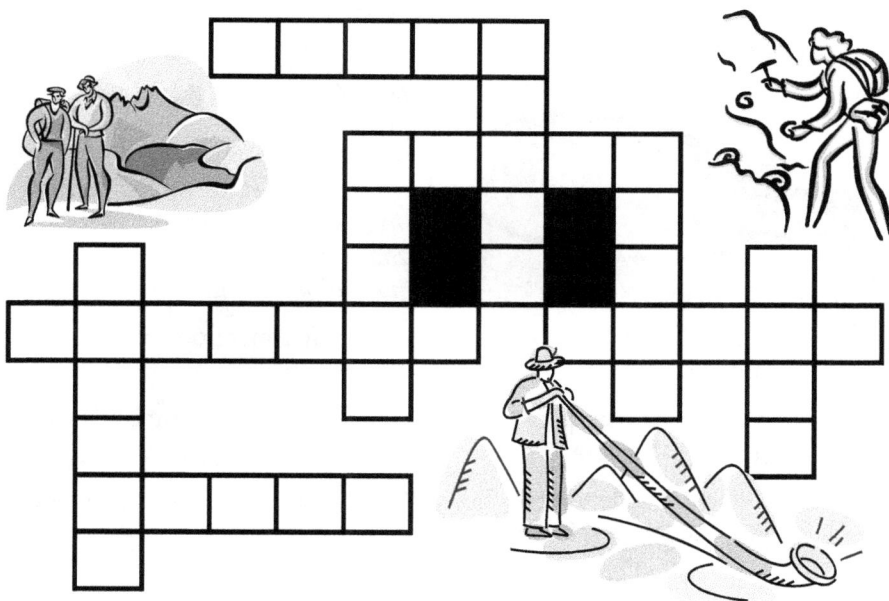

We thank You Lord for the majesty of the mountains and the grace of the hills around us. May they continue to inspire us and bring us closer to you in our daily lives. In Christ's name we pray. Amen.

Young Searchers

By Andrew and Andrea Marple

Fish in the Bible

Do you know how many different kinds of fish are mentioned in the Bible? It's a trick question really, as no type of fish is actually referred to by name.

Having said that, fish are mentioned very often in both the Old and New Testaments.

Fish in the Old Testament

The first reference to fish in the Bible is in the very first chapter of Genesis, verse 26:

*Then God said, "Let us make man in our image, in our likeness, and let them rule over the **fish** of the sea and the birds of the air, over the livestock, over all the earth, and over all the creatures that move along the ground."*

Look up the following references to study further mentions of fish in the Old Testament:

1. The first of the plagues on the Egyptians in the time of Moses (Exodus 7:18).

2. Moses wonders how he will feed an army of six hundred thousand men (Numbers 11:22).

3. A prophecy about Egypt (Isaiah 9-11).

4. The Israelites depended on trade with foreigners (Nehemiah 3:2-4 and 13:16).

In the law given to the Israelites by God, all fish with fins and scales were regarded as clean and therefore good for eating. Water creatures that did not have fins and scales were regarded as unclean. We can read this in Leviticus 11:9-12.

Visit www.obt.org.uk for more resources

Fish in the New Testament

Moving to the New Testament, fish and fishermen become important parts of the work and teachings of Jesus Christ. Matthew chapter 4:18-22 tells us how He called His first disciples – Peter, Andrew, James and John – all fishermen.

Later on in Matthew 14:13-19, Jesus performs the miracle of feeding the five thousand with only five loaves of bread and two fish. Just as the Gospel message of Jesus Christ can appear insufficient to many people today, we know that there is enough to satisfy everyone who wants to share it.

Fishy Codes!

In the 1st century, the early Christians were persecuted and many were forced to hide away and meet in secret. The symbol of the fish became a favourite image of Jesus Christ that they could use as a code. The Greek word for fish is *ichthus,* which is made up of the first letters of the Greek words that define who Jesus is: **I**hsous **CH**ristos **TH**eou **U**ios **S**wthr = Jesus Christ of God the Son Saviour.

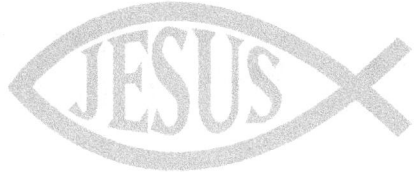

Below is another code that you can break. When completed it details another fish based miracle that Jesus performed:

Break the Code!

	A	B	C	D	E
1	fish	so	large	such	when
2	to	had	done	a	their
3	they	caught	number	nets	they
4	of	that	began	break	

E1 A3 B2 C2 B1 , E3 B3 D1 D2 C1 C3
A4 A1 B4 E2 D3 C4 A2 D4 .

Young Searchers

By Andrew and Andrea Marple

Insects in the Bible

Summer means a variety of things; hot days, barbeques with friends and family, and lazy afternoons in the garden. The warm weather also means that we have to watch out for all those pesky little insects roaming around outside. From microscopic bedbugs to giant cockroaches, there are millions of species of insects in the world. In the UK, insect bites and stings are rarely more than an irritation, but elsewhere in the world insects can pose a significant danger.

Of course, insects were a part of daily life in Biblical times as well and there are a variety of insects mentioned in the Bible. Look up the following verses in an NIV Bible and draw a line to the insect (or insects) mentioned:

Verse	Insects
Proverbs 6:6-8	
1 Kings 8:37	
1 Samuel 24:14	
Psalm 105:34	
Matthew 23:24	
Joshua 24:12	
Jeremiah 46:23	
Psalm 118:12	
Isaiah 7:18	
Exodus 8:16-19	
Joel 1:4	
Ecclesiastes 10:1	

In Matthew 6:19-21, our Lord Jesus Christ mentions an insect – a moth:

Treasures in Heaven

"Do not store up for yourselves treasures on earth, where moth and rust destroy, and where thieves break in and steal. But store up for yourselves treasures in heaven, where moth and rust do not destroy, and where thieves do not break in and steal. For where your treasure is, there your heart will be also."

The word *treasures* conjures up images of pirate chests overflowing with gold coins and precious jewels. We think of long lost hoards of golden objects discovered in Egypt or dug up from the ground after being buried for hundreds of years.

Jesus is telling us not to put too much value on possessions and material things, which can quickly vanish like a moth destroying a piece of material. Instead, we should seek those heavenly treasures that are everlasting and cannot be destroyed, stolen or lost.

Building up treasures in heaven starts with accepting Christ as your personal Lord and Saviour and assuring ourselves of our place with God for eternity. On top of this basis we should add our love of God, the power of prayer, fellowship with other Christians, daily Bible study, bringing others to Christ, and being able to forgive one another as Christ has forgiven us.

If we concentrate on building up earthly treasures through wealth and possessions then that is where our heart will be. However, we want our heart to be for heavenly activities, a heart for Jesus Christ, building up treasures for Him.

Dear Lord,
Guide us in the way that You want us to live our lives. Help us to do those things that are pleasing to You and that build up treasures in Heaven.
In Christ's name we pray, Amen.

Christmas and After Christmas

J	U	D	A	Z	R	U	O	I	V	A	S
B	E	T	H	L	E	H	E	M	Y	N	K
I	P	S	M	L	E	G	N	A	R	G	C
N	H	A	U	G	P	H	E	R	O	D	D
C	E	J	O	S	E	P	H	Y	R	L	L
E	R	L	T	T	H	R	R	Y	M	D	F
N	D	A	S	H	I	E	E	G	O	D	L
S	E	L	B	A	T	S	P	G	H	S	O
E	H	R	O	D	G	R	G	H	N	T	K
K	I	N	O	U	A	T	S	N	E	A	S
M	A	R	N	J	E	M	A	G	I	R	M
C	L	O	T	H	S	N	A	R	Y	K	D

JESUS
ANGEL
MARY
KINGS
HEROD
STABLE
GOLD
MYRRH
JUDAH
CLOTHS
MAGI
STAR

BETHLEHEM   MANGER   INCENSE
JOSEPH   SHEPHERD   SAVIOUR

Young Searchers

By Andrew and Andrea Marple

Joseph and Mary

At the start of the Old Testament, in Genesis Chapter 3, we read how the first man and woman – Adam and Eve – disobeyed God. Their disobedience in the Garden of Eden led to mankind being separated from God.

At the start of the New Testament, we read how another man and woman – Joseph and Mary – obeyed God. Their obedience, followed by the birth of Jesus, played a very important part in God's plan to restore his relationship with mankind. So, let's discover a bit more about who they were:

JOSEPH

Joseph's story is told in Matthew Chapter 1 verse 16 to Chapter 2 verse 23, and Luke Chapter 1 verse 26 to Chapter 2 verse 52. Please read these passages and answer the following questions:

1. Where did Joseph live? (Luke Ch.1 v.26)

2. Which two well-known Old Testament characters is he descended from? (Matt. 1 v.17)

3. How is Joseph described in Matthew Ch. 1 v.19?

4. When God appeared to Joseph in a dream (Matt. Ch.1 v.20), what did He tell him about Mary and the son she was to have?

MARY

Mary's story is told throughout the Gospels. Please read Luke Chapter 1 verses 26 to 37.

1. Where did Mary live? (Luke Ch. 1 v.26)

2. What was her relationship to Joseph? (v.27)

3. Mary is described as "highly favoured" (v.28) and again as having "found favour with God" (v.30), why?

Mary's life was about to change forever. When the angel Gabriel told her the baby would be God's Son, Mary's answer was one that God had been waiting in vain to hear from so many other people:

v.38: "I am _____," Mary answered.
"May it be _____."
Then the angel left her.

Mary knew God was asking her to serve Him and she willingly obeyed. Help Joseph and Mary to find their way from Nazareth to Bethlehem below:

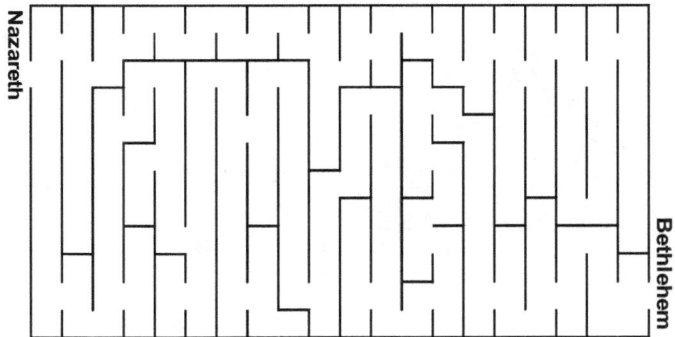

Joseph and Mary's willingness to trust and accept God's message made it possible for the birth of God's promised Saviour – the Messiah, Jesus. Our separation from God, which began in the Garden of Eden, could have continued forever. However, this was never what God had in mind. His desire has always been for mankind to have a close and loving relationship with Him. Through Jesus' birth, God found a way to mend our separation from Him. It is through Jesus that we have a way back to God and Christmas is the time we celebrate the fulfilment of this wonderful plan.

Published by The Open Bible Trust

Young Searchers

By Andrew and Andrea Marple

Can't see the wood for the trees?

Have you ever heard this expression used? What might it mean? Perhaps it means that we're busy looking at the overall picture without seeing what's really in there. In other words, we're looking at the trees but forgetting the wood or the substance that they're made of.

Could this be applied to Christmas?

Have you noticed how some shops decorate Christmas trees from as early as November, using the attraction of sparkles, glitter and tinsel as people turn their attention to the big picture of Christmas? But what have trees, snow and tinsel really got to do with Jesus being born?

We can all enjoy the build up to December 25th, but are the trees hiding the wood for us?

What should we be seeing this Christmas?

The best way to focus on the real message of Christmas is by reading our Bible. Let's do that now to fill in the missing branches of our own tree.

Clue 1 – The area of Israel in which Jesus was born. Clue 2 – "Today in the town of David a Saviour has been born to ___;" (Luke Ch.2 v.11). Clue 3 across – The Magi followed this to find the baby Jesus. Clue 3 down – The first group of visitors to the baby Jesus. Clue 4 – There was no room here for Mary and Joseph. Clue 5 – Who told clue 3 down to go to the stable?. Clue 6 – "I bring you good news of great __ that will be for all people." (Luke Ch.2 v.10). Clue 7 – Who had to go to Bethlehem to take part in a census? Clue 8 – The king of clue 1. Clue 9 – Where did the angel tell Joseph to go to, to escape from clue 8?

But don't just read your Bible at Christmas – let's make it our New Year's resolution to daily read God's word to continually seek the truths that it contains. Have a very happy Christmas and be sure not to miss the wood amongst all the trees.

Young Searchers

By Andrew and Andrea Marple

Seeing Stars

At Christmas time they are everywhere: shiny, sparkling, brilliant white; decorating shop windows, placed proudly on top of Christmas trees and peeping through the stable window of every picture of the baby asleep in his manger. Yes, of course, it is the Star of Bethlehem.

Bethlehem was the small town, about five miles south of Jerusalem, where Jesus was born. Matthew chapter 2 tells us of the star that guided the Wise Men to Him. Read the whole of the chapter and then try to fill in the missing words from the following verses:

Verse 1 – "Jesus was born in Bethlehem in _____ , during the time of King _____ …".

Verse 2 – "Where is the one who has been born _____ of the _____?"

Verse 10 – "When they saw the _____, they were _____ ".

Verse 11 – "They saw the child with his mother _____, and they bowed down and _____ him."

Verse 13 – "Take the child and his mother and escape to _____."

So who were the Wise Men?

Not very much is really known about these people. They were probably astrologers (people who try to predict what happens on earth, by studying the stars and planets – not to be confused with astronomers). Tradition says that they came from near Babylon, which was in modern day Iraq. They were probably not kings and nowhere in the Bible does it say that there were three of them. However, they did bring three gifts (can you remember what these were?) so perhaps it was one gift each.

And what was the star they were following?

Some people think that the Star of Bethlehem was formed when the planets of Jupiter, Saturn and Mars all lined up, to give the impression of one very big, bright star. Other people have other explanations, but we must remember that God created the entire universe and might simply have created a new star to announce the birth of His son.

What can we learn from the Star of Bethlehem and the Wise Men?

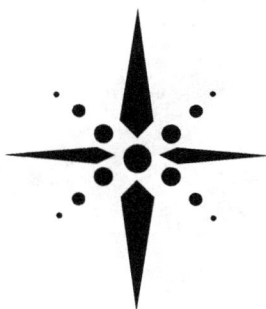

Today, many people are happy just to sit back and wait for God to come to them and offer them gifts. Fewer and fewer people are even prepared to go the short distance to their local church to look for Him. Compare this with the Wise Men, who travelled thousands of miles, on what must have been a very dangerous journey. They were searching for the Son of God, guided by the Star of Bethlehem. When they eventually found Him, they were overcome with joy and showered Him with expensive gifts.

So today, we must all make our own search for the Son of God. We don't have any stars to guide us, but we do have the Bible, the church and Christian friends and relatives.

Dear Father God,

We thank You for the gift of Your Son, our Lord and Saviour. Help us to be wise, like those men of old, who followed Your star. Help us to find Jesus Christ in our own lives and to keep Him there.

In Christ's name we pray.

Amen.

   Published by The Open Bible Trust

Young Searchers

By Andrew and Andrea Marple

Wonderful

Christmas means many things to many people. It can be exciting, stressful, joyous, lonely, expensive. However, on a positive note and as that popular Christmas song keeps telling us, to a lot of people "It's the most **wonderful** time of the year".

When we look in the dictionary, there are two meanings given for "wonderful":

5. Giving a feeling of wonder or astonishment.

6. Something that is extremely fine or excellent.

As we read the Gospel accounts of the birth of Jesus Christ, which we are celebrating now at Christmas, there are a number of passages for which the first meaning is appropriate – they fill us full of wonder. Over the next few weeks in the lead-up to Christmas, why not read through the gospel accounts of Jesus' birth in Matthew (1:18 to 2:23) and Luke (1:26 to 2:20). Make a list of everything that strikes you as wonderful. Here are some ideas below:

How Wonderful that...

Wise Men came from far away.

Jesus and His family escaped from Herod.

A bright star shone over the stable.

Angels appeared.

Lowly shepherds were the first to visit.

The Son of God was born in a stable.

Complete the words in the "wonderful" puzzle below:

Clue		
Led by the star:	**W**	
Jesus' earthly father:	**O**	
Told the Shepherds:	**N**	
Shared the stable:	**D**	
Visted the stable:	**E**	
Jesus' mother:	**R**	
Brought by wisemen:	**F**	
What the inn was:	**U**	
One of the gifts:	**L**	

It could be that we have experienced so many retellings of the Christmas story – at church, school nativity plays, on the television – that there is a danger of losing the great wonder involved. This year, this busy Christmas, whatever your circumstances, let's try and hear the account of Jesus' birth as if for the very first time. With fresh enthusiasm, take time to reflect on all the many wonders that it holds.

The birth of Jesus Christ was truly wonderful in both meanings of the word. The most wonderful thing of all is that God sent His only son, our Lord and Saviour Jesus Christ, to save us, His people.

Dear Lord,

Please help us at this time of Christmas to feel anew the many wonders of the story of the birth of your Son. Give us also the opportunities and the confidence to share this wonderful news with others.

In Christ's name we pray, Amen.

Young Searchers

By Andrew and Andrea Marple

Keeping Christ in Christmas

The Christmas festival is celebrated the world over on December 25th. Yet there seems to be a certain amount of ambiguity and confusion in people's minds over Christmas and its meaning.

Some people feel it is an exclusively Christian holiday and as such has no special meaning for them. Our local schools avoid using the word "Christmas" at all; refering to the holidays as the" Winter Break". Others feel that what should be a holy day has turned into a revelry of over indulgence. A festival of eating and drinking to excess. There is also the issue of how commercial Christmas has become, with overwhelming enticements to spend, spend, spend!

However, regardless of any ambiguous feelings, I suspect not many of us would actually be willing to give up the Christmas holidays!

Searching for the meaning of Christmas.

The very word itself gives us a hint as to the origins of Christmas. It started with the birth of Jesus Christ over 2000 years ago, in the country of Israel. He was a gift of love from God; "…and you shall name him Jesus (meaning "saviour"), for he will save his people from their sins." (Matt.1:21)

So What?

In today's society it doesn't seem to be enough to know the true meaning of Christmas."So what?" is the response to trying to bring Jesus' birth into the party season. Yet we need to keep the celebrations of peace, love and joy connected to Jesus. Our feelings of good will towards ourselves and each other need to come from hearts that are convinced of the importance of Jesus' birth. Feelings of fear and uncertainty can give way to joy when we remember that Jesus was sent by God to be the King of Kings- incomparable with anyone before or after. We can trust him with our lives because he came to be our Saviour.

Keeping Christ in Christmas

Christmas will be special in different ways for each of us, depending on our various traditions, customs and memories. Christians can participate in the rituals of the season whilst at the same time keeping Christ as the source of love and light in our hearts. Little things like: sending cards that have a Christian message; having a Nativity scene as a focal point in the home; getting involved in a good- will charity project; being sure to attend Christmas services and setting aside time to read the Christmas story afresh each year.

We are called to trust Jesus and listen to his voice through all the distractions at Christmas. Keep Christ in Christmas so that the joy that is associated with the birth of Jesus can be renewed each year.

> **Thank You Lord for the true meaning of Christmas – the birth of Your Son, our Lord Jesus Christ, sent to be our Saviour. Help us to keep close to you during the season's festivities and maintain our Christian traditions this Christmas.**
>
> **In Christ's name we pray. Amen.**

Young Searchers

By Andrew and Andrea Marple

What's Left after Christmas?

What *was* left when the hosts of angels had returned to their heavenly realms?

When the shepherds had returned to their flocks of sheep?

What *is* left when the last needle-less Christmas tree is dumped by the side of the road?

When the batteries run out on your favourite Christmas present?

What *was* left when the Wise Men returned home to the east?

When the animals in that stable settled down in the straw to rest?

What *is* left when the final Christmas party fades into the night?

When the turkey carcass is cast into the bin?

What *was* left when Mary and Joseph fell exhaustedly to sleep?

What *is* left when we take down the Christmas cards?

The infant Jesus *was* **left**, His glorious life and death, bringing hope to us all, still before Him.

Jesus Christ *is* **left**, as strong a presence in our lives as ever, His resurrection sealing our new life in Him.

Enjoy Christmas this year and celebrate with Christians throughout the world the birth of our Lord and Saviour Jesus Christ. When it's all over, continue to make Him the priority in your lives, because **He** *is* always with us.

Christmas Crossword

Read through the clues for this Christmas crossword and look up the Bible quotations from the Gospels of Matthew and Luke.

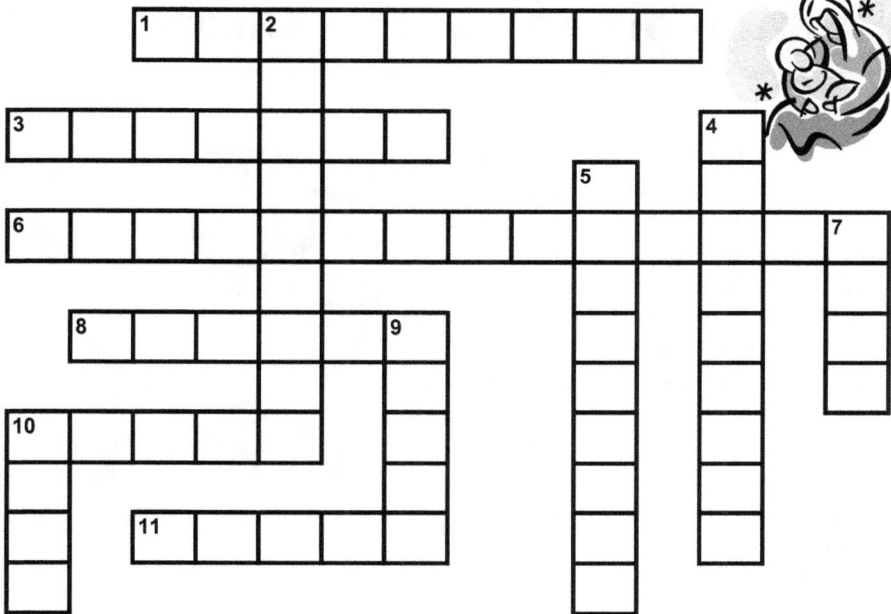

Across

1. The first group of people to visit the stable after Jesus' birth (Luke 2:15)

3. The angel sent to Mary to foretell the birth of Jesus Christ (Luke 1:26)

6. The Roman Emperor at the time of Jesus' birth (Luke 2:1) (6,8)

8. The husband of Mary (Matt 1:19)

10. A gift from the Wise Men (Matt 2:11)

11. The house and line to which Joseph belonged (Luke 2:4)

Down

2. Relative of Mary and mother of John the Baptist (Luke 1:36)

4. Birthplace of Jesus Christ (Luke 2:4)

5. The governor of Syria at the time of Jesus' birth (Luke 2:2)

7. This guided the Wise Men to the birthplace of Jesus (Matt 2:9)

9. The King of Judea at the time of Jesus' birth (Matt 2:3)

10. The Wise men who came from the east to worship Jesus (Matt 2:1)

Young Searchers

By Andrew and Andrea Marple

What's our focus this Christmas?

During the past year we have become an Auntie and Uncle again, this time to two lovely nieces. We eagerly awaited their births: praying for safe deliveries, wondering who they'd look like, and when we'd be able to visit them first for a cuddle etc. Now that they've arrived, life for their parents is all about feeding, doctor's appointments and establishing a comfortable routine for the family. The focus is on the present and the joys and challenges that have been presented by their tiny, new lives.

At Christmas the Nativity picture focuses on a baby. The birth of Jesus was also eagerly awaited; ever since the angel Gabriel told Mary,

"…you have found favour with God. You will be with child and give birth to a son, and you are to give him the name Jesus." (Luke ch.1 v.30-31)

Like in any pregnancy, the lead-up to Jesus' birth would also have been an anxious time, especially when the due date coincided with a journey to Bethlehem for a Roman census.

It's easy to look at the baby Jesus on our Christmas cards, Advent calendars and school nativity tableaus and see just a cute baby born in extraordinary circumstances. Yes, Jesus was that child in a manger but, unlike with other births, it wasn't then all about the everyday marvels of

Visit www.obt.org.uk for more resources

a new-born; the routine of feeds, nappy changes, "cooing" and "ahhing" and wondering who he'd look like.

For Christians, God's focus for us is much bigger than this. Remember, Jesus did not come into being when he was born because he is eternal. John ch.1 vs1-2 say "**Before anything else existed, there was Christ, with God. He has always been alive and is himself God.**" (Life Application Bible) The birth of Jesus is about the awesome fact that Jesus never ceased to be the eternal God who has always existed. Before the world began he lived with God. He is unique as God's special son yet he *is* God-completely human *and* completely divine;

"For in Christ all the fullness of the Deity lives in bodily form" (Col. Ch.2 v.9)

Mary, as she cradled her newborn baby in her arms in the stable, although living in the present moment of excitement and joy, must have looked at Jesus with her mind filled with so much more than the sleeping and feeding routine to come, the first smile and "terrible two's" tantrum. The Angel Gabriel had from the start told her…

"He will be great and will be called the Son of the Most High. The Lord God will give him the throne of his father David, and he will reign over the house of Jacob for ever; his kingdom will never end."
(Luke ch.1 vs. 32-33)

So, while babies are a lovely focus, a blessing and a challenge, *our challenge* this Christmas is to see in baby Jesus God's plan for mankind;

"Today in the town of David a Saviour has been born to you; he is Christ the Lord." (Luke ch.2 v.11).

                    Published by The Open Bible Trust

Young Searchers

By Andrew and Andrea Marple

Don't Forget your Manners!

Can you think back to Christmas morning? What did you do when you first set eyes on each new gift just for you? After the "Wow, this is great…can I try it out now?" or "Can you help me set it up?" we hope you remembered to say, "Thank you".

As the festive season wore on, did you have to 'phone round your relatives to say "Thanks", or even worse, have to write a letter? Maybe we get fed up of saying "Thank you" because we're not used to doing it so often and it interferes with the time we want to spend enjoying the gifts. But if we don't show our appreciation we seem ungrateful and that upsets the giver.

Some people in the Bible were ungrateful:

Using your Bible can you find Luke chapter 17 and read verses 11 to 19. In this passage:

1. Who is the giver? _____
2. What is the gift? _____
3. How many received Jesus' gift? _____
4. How many men are grateful enough to say "Thank you"? _____
5. What does Jesus think about this? (vs. 17 and 18)_____

Now find Numbers chapter 11 and read verses 4 to 6. When Moses rescued the Israelites from the Egyptians he led them to a safe place where they were free from slavery. God provided food from heaven called manna. But:

1. What gift had the Israelites already received? _____
2. Who was the giver? _____
3. While these people were concentrating on their stomachs, what had they forgotten about? _____

Some people in the Bible were grateful:

Can you now look up the following passages to find
out who DID remember to say "Thank you":

1. _____ gave thanks over the birth of
   a son (1 Samuel chapter 1 verse 27 to chapter
   2 verse 2).
2. Daniel thanked God for _____ and
   _____ (Daniel chapter 2, verse
   23).
3. _____ gave thanks over bread and fish (John chapter 6
   verses 10 and 11).
4. _____ gave thanks in the temple when Jesus was first
   brought there (Luke chapter 2 verses 36 to 38).
5. _____ gave thanks because she had found favour with
   God (Luke chapter 1 verses 46 to 55).

Do you thank God for His gifts to you?

In Ephesians chapter 5, verse 20, Paul writes that we should be "always
giving thanks to God the Father for everything, in the name of our Lord
Jesus Christ". God has given us so much to be grateful for. It pleases
Him when we are thankful. Just as God knew the needs of the Biblical
characters you've just read about, He knows about **our needs** too. One of
the best ways to thank Him is through our prayers. As the hymn says,
"Give thanks with a grateful heart".

Just as we need to thank our parents, relatives and friends for all those
Christmas gifts, we need to remember our heavenly Father has also given
us so many good things. Take a moment to think about God's gifts to you
in your life. Perhaps you could use this prayer:

> **Thank You Lord that You know my needs. Help me
> to be grateful for what I have and to know that
> everything comes from You. I thank You for your
> many gifts to me.**
> **I pray this in Christ's name. Amen.**

          Published by The Open Bible Trust

Young Searchers

By Andrew and Andrea Marple

Angels

Did you see a nativity play this Christmas, maybe at your school or church? If you did, can you remember what the angels looked like? They are normally dressed in white, with wings, and tinsel on their heads. But do you think angels really look like this and have you ever stopped to wonder what their purpose is in God's plan?

Angels are not human beings like us, so we all have difficulty trying to imagine what they must be like. Let's see what the Bible says.

What are angels?

They are a special creation of beings that live in Heaven with God. Read one verse of Paul's letter to Timothy (1 Timothy Ch.5, v.21) to see whom he groups together with God and Christ Jesus. However, although angels are given a high, "exalted" position, Hebrews Ch.1 makes it clear that they are not as important as Jesus. Verse 4 says:

> "So he (the Son) became as much superior to the angels as the name he has inherited is superior to theirs".

What do they look like?

Turn in your Bible to Matthew Ch.28 and read verses 1 to 7. Copy out verse 3:

_____

_____

_____

What do angels do?

Living in the immediate presence of God, it is as though their white, shining appearance is reflecting something of the glory of God. Read the parable of the lost coin, Luke Ch.15, v.8-10. What do the angels do in verse 10 and why?

Now turn to Hebrews Ch.1, v.6. We find that "... all God's angels _____ _____".

The Bible records a number of people who met angels. Read the following passages to see **who** they were and **how** they reacted:

	Who?	How?
Luke Ch.1, v.11-12		
Luke Ch.1, v.28-30		
Luke Ch.2, v.9-10		

What was the common reaction to seeing or hearing these angels? Yes, they were afraid. But do you remember what the angel said in each case? "do not fear". It seems that the one thing we can be sure about angels is that we don't need to be frightened of them.

"The angels are only spirit messengers sent out to help
and care for those who are to receive his salvation"
Hebrews Ch.1,v.14 (Life Application Bible).

O Lord, thank you that angels are Your special messengers in the Bible. Help us to worship and praise You continually as the angels do. Although we cannot understand exactly how they help and care for Christians, thank you that Your angels are with us each day.
We pray these things in Christ's name. Amen.

Easter

G	O	L	G	J	R	C	B	C	R	T	N
O	E	S	O	U	E	A	M	U	A	O	E
G	T	T	L	D	S	P	O	H	I	M	P
O	A	O	H	A	S	I	T	X	R	E	S
L	L	N	D	S	V	A	I	A	C	A	A
G	I	E	O	A	E	F	B	S	H	S	B
O	P	R	S	D	I	M	D	P	R	N	B
T	C	S	O	C	Y	R	A	M	O	R	A
H	T	O	U	R	A	I	Z	N	S	O	R
A	L	R	M	U	A	M	A	Y	E	H	A
B	C	N	G	C	H	R	I	S	T	T	B
N	O	I	T	C	E	R	E	U	S	E	R

JUDAS
DEATH
TOMB
PILATE
BLOOD
CHRIST
GUARDS
CROSS
MARY
STONE
THORNS
SAVIOUR

GETHSEMANE **CRUCIFIXION** **CAIAPHAS**
GOLGOTHA **RESURRECTION** **BARABBAS**

                    Published by The Open Bible Trust

Young Searchers

By Andrew and Andrea Marple

A Matter of Life and Death

At Easter time we remember the death of Jesus Christ on the cross and his resurrection (coming back to life). It's important to remember that these two go together. Instead of death coming after life, life now comes after death. Why are Christ's death and resurrection important for us?

Jesus died for us:

All four gospels tell us about the death of Jesus. Use your Bibles to find the missing words on the cross.

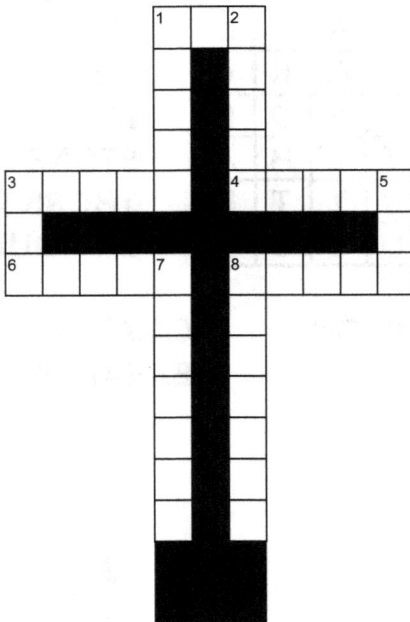

Across

1. '..."You who are going to destroy the temple and build it in three days, save yourself! Come down from the cross, if you are the ___ of God!"' Matt 27:40.

3. 'Then _____ remembered the word the Lord had spoken to him: 'Before the cock crows today, you will disown me three times.' Luke 22:61.

4. 'When _____ saw Jesus, he was greatly pleased, because for a long time he had been wanting to see him.' Luke 23:8.

6. '...Jesus came out wearing the crown of _____s and the purple robe..' John 19:5.

8. 'And when Jesus had cried out again in a loud _____, he gave up his spirit.' Matt 27:50.

Down

1. '...one of the soldiers pierced Jesus' side with a _____ ' John 19:34
2. 'About the _____ hour Jesus cried out in a loud voice, "Eloi, Eloi, lama Sabachthani?" – which means, "My God, my God, why have you forsaken me?" Matt 27:46.
3. 'The soldiers twisted together a crown of thorns and _____ it on his head.' John 19:2.
5. 'And when the centurion, who stood there in front of Jesus, heard his cry and saw how he _____d, he said, "Surely this man was the Son of God!".' Mark 15:39.
7. '...this man (Jesus) has done _____ wrong.' Luke 23:41.
8. 'One man ran, filled a sponge with wine _____, put it on a stick, and offered it to Jesus to drink.' Mark 15:36.

Christ's death happened because of sin in the world. None of us are perfect, we all do, think and say wrong things and are therefore "sinners". The Bible tells us that our sins separate us from God (Isaiah 59:2-3). However, because of God's great love for us he sent Jesus into the world to deal with the problem of our sin and pay the price for it. The only way to do this was by dying in our place on the cross. John 3:16 –

> ## "For God so loved the world that he gave his one and only Son, that whoever believes in him shall not perish but have eternal life"

Jesus Rose Again

After three days Jesus rose again. He lives for evermore and we know that death has finally been conquered. When we believe this as Christians, we know that we too will rise again after death to live a new life with God in heaven.

> I thank You Lord that You loved me enough to send Jesus to take the blame for my sins. I know that He is alive today. Please help me to let him into my heart.
> I pray this in Christ's name. Amen.

Young Searchers

By Andrew and Andrea Marple

Hands

As far back in our lives as we can remember, our hands have been very important to us. From early childhood, reaching out for a toy or biscuit, to holding on to a swing and gripping a pencil. We use our hands all the time and they help us achieve wonderful things, from typing e-mails to creating paintings and music.

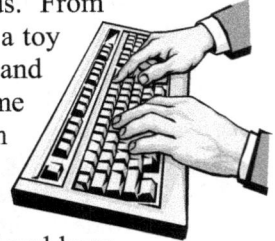

Here are some Biblical passages that mention hands. Read them to see which people are involved and how hands played a part in their stories:

1. Exodus Ch. 17, v. 10-13

_____ and _____ held up Moses' hands when he grew tired.

2. Genesis Ch. 27, v. 21-24

_____ had very hairy hands. His brother Jacob had smooth hands and covered them with goatskin to trick their blind father.

3. Exodus Ch. 14, v. 21-28

_____ twice stretched out his hand over the Red Sea. The first time, the sea parted and the Israelites escaped and crossed through dry land. The second time, the water flowed back, and the pursuing Egyptians all drowned.

4. 2 Timothy Ch. 1, v. 2-6

By laying his hands on Timothy, _____ was used by God to pass on gifts of the Holy Spirit. These were to help Timothy to serve the church.

5. John Ch. 13, v. 6-9

When Jesus washed his feet, _____ asked for his hands and body also to be washed.

6. Matthew Ch. 27, v. 11-26

In the lead up to the death of Jesus, we read that _____, finding nothing to accuse Jesus of, literally washed his hands of Him.

And finally we get to the hands of Jesus. Throughout His ministry, they brought healing and blessing to many people. In Matthew Ch. 8, v. 1-3, we read how a man with leprosy was healed; "Jesus reached out His hand and touched the man … Immediately he was cured of his leprosy."(v.3)

The same hands that Jesus used to bless and to heal were used to nail him to a cross at His *death*. And these are the same hands that Thomas saw as proof of Jesus' *resurrection*:

Then He said to Thomas, "Put your finger here; see my hands. Reach out your hand and put it into my side. Stop doubting and believe." (John Ch. 20, v. 27).

Thank You for our hands Lord. Help us to use them to do good for You. Thank You for Your hands. You used them to bless and heal many and through Your death on the cross, our sins have been forgiven. We pray this in Christ's name. Amen.

Young Searchers

By Andrew and Andrea Marple

A Heart Full of Love

St.Valentine's Day is a special day for declaring our love for each other. Did you get carried away by the occasion? Was sending a card not enough? Were you coaxed into buying flowers, chocolates and the cute teddy bear as well? Maybe, maybe not, but I bet you signed the card – after all, if you've gone to all that trouble you want to be sure that they know it's you who loves them!

Well, it was only recently whilst researching for a school assembly that I found out a bit more about the story of Saint Valentine.

It is thought that Valentine was a Christian in Rome around 1,700 years ago. This was at the time when the Roman emperors were killing Christians for their beliefs. It is thought that Valentine was a leader in the church, possibly a priest. He preached about Jesus Christ and many people who heard him became Christians.

Because of this, the Roman emperor threw Valentine into prison. But this did not stop him telling other people about Christ and even some of the prison guards became Christians. Finally, the emperor could stand this no longer and had Valentine killed.

So why did Valentine go through all that suffering and refuse to stop talking about Christ? After all, had he stopped, he could have lived longer and even been a free man. Perhaps, once you've solved the puzzle on the next page, you will be able to understand a bit better.

Break the Code!

	A	B	C	D
1	love	one	than	he
2	that	greater	his	for
3	lay	this	has	friends
4	no	life	down	his

B2 A1 C3 A4 B1 C1 B3 , A2 D1

---   ,   -----------------

A3 C4 D4 B4 D2 C2 D3 .

---   .

Do you see that Valentine was acting out of love for his fellow humans? He gave his life in order to share his belief in Jesus.

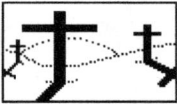 No one is sure whether these details of Valentine's life are true. But if they are, as a Christian, surely he took his inspiration from his Lord and Saviour Jesus Christ, who had given His own life on the cross some 300 years earlier. How much greater though was the sacrifice Christ made and how much deeper was the love He had for us! Christ died to save all those who believe in Him throughout the whole world: past, present and future.

> ## "For God so loved the world that he gave his one and only Son, that whoever believes in him shall not perish but have eternal life"
>
> ### John Ch.3 v.16

Young Searchers

By Andrew and Andrea Marple

He is alive!

At **Easter**, we remember the death of our Lord Jesus Christ on the cross at Calvary – His **crucifixion**. Take yourself back two thousand years and try to imagine how the disciples, the family of Jesus and all His many followers must have felt after this event.

They must have been feeling terrible. All the hopes and dreams that they had built up so recently had seemingly come to nothing. Their lives, which had been filled with the presence of Jesus Christ, were now empty and they were sad, desperate and fearful for the future.

Then suddenly came the wonderful news that the tomb where Jesus' body had been laid, after His crucifixion, was empty; Christ had risen from the dead. At first they perhaps thought that this was a rumour, the news was really too good to be true. But no, Christ really was alive again and the Bible records the evidence. Read the following passages and note down the names of those to whom the risen Jesus Christ appeared:

Appearances of Jesus Christ after His Resurrection

Matt 28:9	T			■	W									
Matt 28:17	E					■	D							
Mark 16:9	M			■	M									
Luke 24:15	T		■	T										
Luke 24:34	S				■	P								
1 Cor 15:6	F			■	H									
1 Cor 15:7	J													
1 Cor 15:7	T		■											
1 Cor 15:7	P		■											

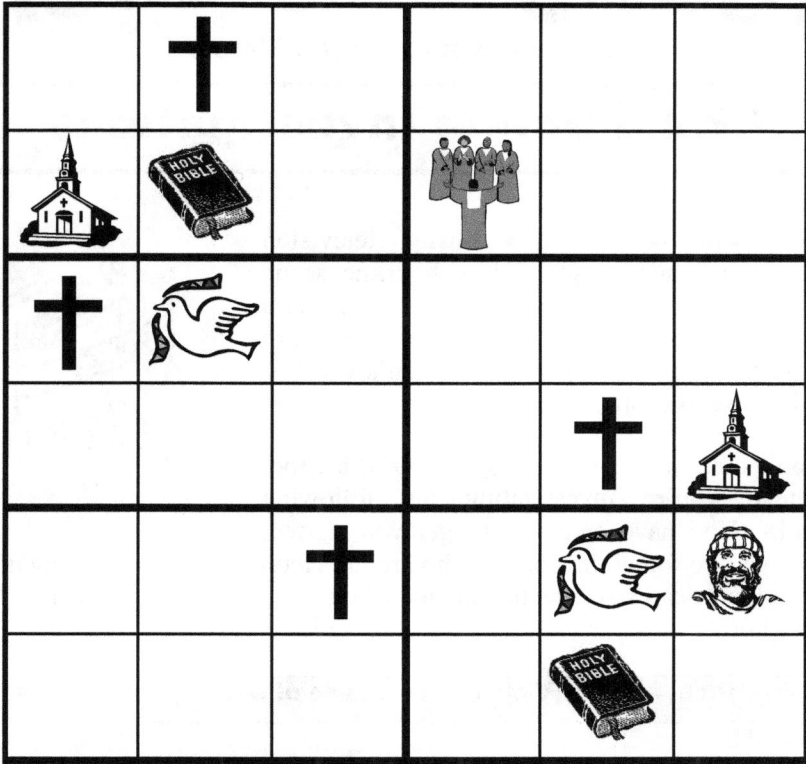

Young Searchers Sudoku

Complete the grid; every row, column
and mini-grid must contain each of the six pictures.

We all have times in our lives when we are feeling sad, desperate or fearful for the future. Continuing to **trust** in God and seek His guidance through **prayer** will help us through these difficulties. The same joy that the people experienced when they heard the news of Jesus' resurrection from the dead is available to all of us through faith. All we need to do is to believe that the Lord Jesus is **alive** today.

Young Searchers

By Andrew and Andrea Marple

Crime Scene Investigations

Have you noticed how many television programmes nowadays deal with crime scene investigations and dead bodies? Clues and forensic evidence is pieced together to learn about the final moments of a person's life and their cause of death.

People died in all sorts of ways in the Bible too. Pretend you're investigating the following deaths. You have evidence to get you started.

Now you've found the bodies, who are the victims and how did they die? Were their deaths accidental, suicide or murder? Who is responsible for the crimes?

Evidence	Victim	Cause of Death	Who did it?
Acts 7:59			
Matt.14:10			
Gen.4:8			
II Kings 9: 33-37			
Judg.16:28-30			
II Sam.18:9-15			
Esther 7:6-10			
Acts 5:3-5			
Matt.27:1-5			
II Sam.6:6-7			
Judg.4:17-22			
I Sam.4:12-18			
Matt.27:35-37			

If you want your investigation to be really thorough, you could even try and find out *why* each of these Biblical characters died.

For the final entry in the table, the **victim** was our Lord Jesus Christ. The cause of death was crucifixion and he was put to death by the Romans. It is the most important of them all and the most significant for us today. John 3:16 tells us **why** it happened:

"For God so loved the world that he gave his one and only Son that whoever believes in him shall not perish but have eternal life".

As an investigator, would you have concluded that this death was no accident, murder or suicide? It was God's will.

Jesus sacrificed himself for others and, unlike the other deaths, he rose again victorious three days later.

During this joyful Easter season of new life and renewal, let's celebrate the central event of our faith – the Resurrection of our Lord and Saviour Jesus Christ.

The message of Easter is the message of the Risen Lord, of his triumph over sin and death. It is a permanent message of hope for the world.

For the full facts of this "case", why don't you investigate for yourself in Matt 26-27, Mark 14-16, Luke 22-24 and John 18-20.

> We thank you Lord God, that Your son Jesus Christ rose from death on the cross to the triumph of a Saviour's resurrection. For You so loved the world that You gave us, and other sinners, the hope of eternal life. In Christ's name we pray, Amen.

Young Searchers

By Andrew and Andrea Marple

Riding on a Donkey

Have you ever ridden on a donkey? I remember seaside holidays when I was young and a real treat was to ride on a donkey along the beach. But our own Lord and Saviour Jesus Christ also rode on a donkey. Let's read the Gospel of Mark chapter 11, verses 1 to 11.

We are told that Jesus entered the city of Jerusalem riding on a donkey's colt. This animal would have been slightly larger than the ones we are used to seeing at the seaside. Besides carrying people, donkeys were used for ploughing, carrying heavy loads and turning millstones to make flour.

You might have expected the Lord Jesus Christ to make a grand entrance into Jerusalem, accompanied by many people, wearing the finest clothes and seated on a fabulous horse. Instead Jesus showed his humility and identified himself with the ordinary people of the city and their everyday problems.

If the people of Jerusalem had known their Bible, however, they would not have been surprised at the manner of Christ's entrance. This was exactly as prophesised in the Old Testament in Zechariah 9:9:

Rejoice greatly, O Daughter of Zion!
Shout, Daughter of Jerusalem!
See, your king comes to you,
righteous and having salvation,
gentle and riding on a donkey,
on a colt, the foal of a donkey.

Visit www.obt.org.uk for more resources

Try this biblical donkey crossword:

Clues Across: 1. Although the donkey knew its owner's manger, who did not understand? (Isaiah 1:3)   **5.** Who heard some good news whilst looking for his father's donkey? (1 Samuel 9)   **6.** Who obeyed God, taking his son and donkey up a mountain? (Genesis 22)   **7.** Which disobedient king was forced to live with wild donkeys? (Daniel 5:21)   **9.** What noise does Job say a wild donkey makes? (Job 6:5)   **10.** How does Zechariah describe the one who would come riding on a donkey? (Zechariah 9:9)

Clues Down: 2. Who struck down a thousand men with the jawbone of a donkey? (Judges 15:15)   **3.** Whose donkey saw an angel of the Lord? (Numbers 22:23)   **4.** People threw these on to the road in front of the Lord Jesus on his donkey (Mark 11:8)   **8.** People used these instead of a saddle for the Lord Jesus on his donkey (Mark 11:7)

The most solemn week of the Christian year – Holy Week – is the week leading up to Easter. Holy Week begins on Palm Sunday when we commemorate Christ's triumphant arrival in Jerusalem to the cheers of the crowd, riding on a donkey.

Sports

L	O	O	P	Y	R	E	K	O	O	N	S
F	O	O	T	B	A	L	L	L	S	E	S
E	F	L	O	G	J	U	D	O	C	N	C
N	E	S	Q	U	A	S	H	P	I	O	I
C	Y	Y	C	R	I	C	K	E	T	T	T
I	R	E	D	Y	B	O	W	L	S	N	E
N	E	K	A	O	C	S	E	A	A	I	L
G	H	C	c	R	L	L	G	W	N	M	H
O	C	O	T	E	N	N	I	S	M	D	T
A	R	H	S	P	O	L	O	N	Y	A	A
L	A	S	W	I	M	M	I	N	G	B	T
L	A	B	T	E	N	G	N	I	X	O	B

RUGBY
GOLF
BOXING
TENNIS
JUDO
DARTS
POOL
BOWLS
HOCKEY
CRICKET
POLO
SQUASH

GYMNASTICS   FENCING   SWIMMING
ATHLETICS   ARCHERY   BADMINTON
SNOOKER   FOOTBALL

Published by The Open Bible Trust

Young Searchers

By Andrew and Andrea Marple

Glorious Ambition

Whether or not you're a football fan, you can't help but have noticed that we are in the middle of a huge competition where 32 of the world's nations are doing their utmost to win the World Cup. Whilst most of the countries don't stand a chance of winning, it will be each team's greatest ambition to lift the trophy. A dictionary defines "ambition" as "a strong desire for success or achievement". The likes of David Beckham and Ronaldo are ambitious for sporting success, and if you were to ask any member of the 32 teams taking part in the World Cup what they desired most you could be pretty certain what their answer would be.

This very question was asked to a young king in the Bible who was eager to achieve. His name was Solomon and he had replaced his father David as king of Judah. Being only about 20 years old, it must have been a daunting task. But before his death, his father David had given him some good advice: "I am about to go the way of all the earth," he said. "So be strong, show yourself a man, and observe what the LORD your God requires: Walk in his ways, and keep his decrees and commands, his laws and requirements…"(1 Kings ch. 2, v 2-3).

God was pleased with the way Solomon began his reign as king and in 1 Kings ch.3, v. 5 we read "the LORD appeared to Solomon during the night in a dream." Find this verse in your Bible and fill in what God said next:

"___ ___ _____ ___ ____ __ __ ____ ___"

What Solomon asked for was *wisdom*. His ambition was to succeed in leading his people like his father had, using knowledge, ability and understanding from God. God was pleased he'd not selfishly asked for personal wealth, and gave Solomon knowledge to teach (about plant life, animals, birds, reptiles and fish); ability to speak proverbs and songs; and understanding to discern between right and wrong. More important than this, Solomon's desire was to start building "the temple of the LORD" (as well as a royal palace for himself). He wisely bargained with the king of Tyre, trading wheat and olive oil for the cedar and pine logs and gold he needed. He organised teams of men to quarry and prepare large blocks of quality stone needed to build this magnificent temple. Solomon's ambition to lead wisely resulted in 40 years of successful rule as king over all Israel.

So far, so good, but in this next case, one man's ambition led him to act out of selfish greed. Judas Iscariot was one of Jesus' disciples - a friend. Yet his eagerness for gain led him to betray Jesus by helping the Pharisees to find and arrest him. Having ridden triumphantly into Jerusalem, Jesus knew his betrayal and death were part of God's plan, but as he spent time with his disciples, talking with them and preparing them for his death, he was troubled and upset by Judas' desires: "Jesus was troubled in spirit, and testified, I tell you the truth, one of you is going to betray me". Judas saw an opportunity to make some money from Jesus' death and Satan used his greed to control Judas' actions. Find Luke ch. 22 v. 3 and fill in the missing words:

> "Then Satan entered _ _ _ _ _, called Iscariot, one of the Twelve. And Judas went to the _ _ _ _ _ _ _ _ _ _ _ _ and officers of the temple guard and discussed with them how he might _ _ _ _ _ _ Jesus. They were _ _ _ _ _ _ _ _ _ _ and agreed to give him _ _ _ _ _. He consented and watched for an _ _ _ _ _ _ _ _ _ _ _ to hand _ _ _ _ _ over to them when no crowd was present."

In Matthew's gospel we learn that the successful arrest of Jesus was worth 30 silver coins to Judas.

In today's society we're constantly being told to "always believe in yourself ... follow your dreams and make them happen." Ambition to succeed and achieve in life can be a strong driving force. Whether it's at work, school, home or in sport, it's natural that we want to do our best for our boss, teachers, family, team...for ourselves! As Christians, however, our ambition should go further than this. Our desire needs to be for success and achievement in God's service, believing in His ability to help us.

For our prayer, let us use the words of Colossians ch.1 v. 9-10:

Dear Lord, please give me spiritual wisdom and understanding so that I may know your will for me. Make my desire to know more about You and serve You my greatest ambition.

I pray this in Christ's name. Amen.

Young Searchers

By Andrew and Andrea Marple

Rivals

This summer will see the arrival of the Australian cricket team in England. The rivalry between these two teams, as they battle together to win "The Ashes", will be intense. It is a continuing rivalry that can be dated back to the first match that took place between the two teams in 1877.

Constructive Rivalry

Rivalry can sometimes be a constructive influence on people, motivating them to try harder; to emulate and surpass a competitor. Within the Disciples there was this type of constructive rivalry, each of them inspiring the others in their love and respect for Jesus Christ. In Matthew 26:35 "Peter declared, 'Even if I have to die with you, I will never disown you.' And all the other disciples said the same."

Destructive Rivalry

The Old Testament gives us a number of examples of rivalries where those involved were broken apart and destroyed:

> - **Cain and Abel (Genesis 4)**
> - **Abraham and Lot (Genesis 13)**
> - **Jacob and Esau (Genesis 25 to 35)**

Read these passages and try to answer the following questions:

1. How did the rivalry start?
2. How did this affect the people involved?
3. How did the rivalry end?

Have a go at the word search below, which contains ten alternative words for "rival". It also contains the names of the six rivals from the Old Testament, mentioned earlier:

J	A	C	O	B	E	N	Y	M	E	N	E	Y
R	R	E	E	P	S	O	N	X	R	U	Q	R
O	J	E	Q	O	P	P	O	E	S	A	U	A
T	O	A	D	U	G	O	G	Y	A	E	A	S
I	C	B	A	N	A	N	S	A	R	S	L	R
T	A	R	B	D	E	E	N	I	Y	A	R	E
E	S	A	E	L	O	T	I	P	T	I	O	V
P	I	H	L	S	F	M	N	P	O	I	N	D
M	I	A	M	T	N	E	N	O	P	P	O	A
O	H	M	P	Q	U	P	E	V	C	A	I	N
C	O	N	T	E	S	T	A	N	T	Q	U	S

COMPETITOR   **CONTESTANT**

CHALLENGER   **OPPOSITION**

ADVERSARY   **OPPONENT**

CONTENDER   **EQUAL**

ENEMY   **FOE**

Dear Lord,

Help us to be inspired, challenged and motivated by the good examples of our Christian family and friends. In this way enable us to serve you better in our daily lives.

In Christ's name we pray, Amen.

Young Searchers

By Andrew and Andrea Marple

Compete and Run!

Life is full of competition

From very early on in our lives we've found ourselves having to compete: for our parents' attention over our siblings; for school places; for friends; for popularity and acceptance; to be part of school teams; for university places; for jobs; promotion etc.

The idea of competing is forefront this August as athletes of all nationalities are coming together in Beijing to compete for Olympic glory. The Olympic medals are the prizes for which the athletes are contending. Watching the many events take place, admiring the athletes' focus, determination and stamina from the comfort of our armchairs, we are reminded that Christians are called to train and compete as if in a race too.

Competing for the prize

In the Bible, Paul speaks of the Christian life as a competition; a race.

"Do you not know that in a race all the runners run, but only one gets the prize? Run in such a way as to get the prize. Everyone who competes in the games goes into strict training. They do it to get a crown that will not last; but we do it to get a crown that will last forever. Therefore I do not run like a man running aimlessly; I do not fight like a man beating the air. No I beat my body and make it my slave so that after I have preached to others, I myself will not be disqualified for the prize."
(1 Cor. Ch. 9v.24-27)

Winning a race requires purpose and discipline. Paul used this illustration to explain that the Christian life takes hard work, self-denial and preparation. Just as the Olympians go into "strict training", the Christian's vigour and stamina to "run" through life comes from being equipped with the important disciplines of prayer, Bible study and worship.

Jogging or Running?

Rather than merely watching the race from the stands or jogging along half-heartedly, the Christian is told to **run** as if in a race. In other words it's not enough just to *be* there having made it to the race. "Running aimlessly" won't win us that gold medal. **We have to compete!**

What are we competing with?

These days there are many distractions that cause us to slow down to a gentle jog and take our eyes off the finishing line. Self-indulgence, consumerism and leisure pursuits are just some of the pitfalls we have to contend with, all of which can drain our time, money and resources. At times we will need to give up doing something we want to do in order to do what God wants. Our denial is easier to accept when we have the goal of pleasing God and competing for the eternal reward that is ours.

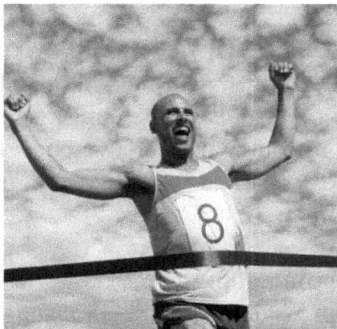

God is our number one supporter throughout our race. He is waiting at the finishing line with our "crown that will last forever", so **RUN!**

Dear Lord,

We thank you that our purpose in life is to run towards You . We pray for discipline in our lives as we compete in the Christian race. We pray for and thank You for Your ongoing encouragement, support and love. In Christ's name we pray. Amen

---

Young Searchers

By Andrew and Andrea Marple

The Race

This summer, athletes from all over the world will be taking part in the Olympic Games in Athens, Greece. This is particularly special, as the first ever Olympic Games were held in Greece in 776 B.C.

The idea of athletes competing would have been familiar to the people of the New Testament and Paul used the picture of an athlete a number of times in his epistles.

Competing for the Prize
"Do you not know that in a race all runners run, but only one gets the prize? Run in such a way as to get the prize."
1 Cor. Ch.9 v.24

What hinders the runner?
"You were running a good race. Who cut in on you and kept you from obeying the truth?"
Gal.Ch.5 v.7

Finishing well
"I have fought the good fight, I have finished the race, I have kept the faith."
2 Tim. Ch.4 v.7

Preparing Ourselves
"Therefore, since we are surrounded by such a great cloud of witnesses, let us throw off everything that hinders and the sin that so easily entangles, and let us run with perseverance the race marked out for us."
Hebrews Ch.12 v.1

Keeping going
"I press on towards the goal to win the prize for which God has called me heavenwards in Christ Jesus." **Phil. Ch.3 v.14**

Winning the race
"Now there is in store for me the crown of righteousness, which the Lord, the righteous Judge, will award to me on that day-and not only to me, but also to all who have longed for his appearing". **2 Tim. Ch.4 v.8**

Visit www.obt.org.uk for more resources

Once we are Christians, we are in the Christian race. God expects us to do our very best. Like the Olympic athletes in Greece this year, we have to prepare, train and exercise diligently. Our preparation to live and run as Christians needs to include prayer, Bible study and worship.

Have you read the parable of the talents? It is found in Matthew Ch. 25 v.14-28. Jesus tells this story to show Christians what we should do with what God has given us. Jesus was most pleased with the man who worked hard and did his best with the excellent resources given to him. He was angry with the man who did nothing and made no effort. Like athletes, Christians are not spectators in the race. Neither are we expected to just stand still.

To win an Olympic medal requires tremendous dedication. Paul used this illustration to show us how we must prepare and train for the Christian life, which he often called a race. As Christians we are running towards our heavenly reward.

Heavenly Father,

We thank you that we are part of the Christian race. We ask that you will enable us to do our best to win this race, through prayer, study and worship. Please help us to make the most of all the many gifts you have given us.

We ask these things in Christ's name. Amen.

Visit www.obt.org.uk for more resources

Christian Life

B	L	P	S	R	E	T	S	I	N	I	M
P	L	L	T	P	E	C	C	A	B	A	H
I	O	A	U	N	I	Y	T	R	E	F	G
H	U	N	M	C	H	R	I	S	T	T	O
S	T	A	J	E	S	C	I	L	O	R	D
W	R	U	N	V	L	L	R	T	E	A	P
O	E	R	G	I	E	E	G	U	N	I	R
L	A	E	S	G	N	O	S	C	H	Y	A
L	C	Y	N	R	N	M	I	S	T	C	I
E	H	A	F	O	R	N	R	I	U	H	S
F	V	R	O	F	G	O	N	A	R	R	E
E	H	P	L	A	W	U	H	T	I	A	F

PRAISE
CHURCH
SONGS
LORD
FAITH
SPIRIT
UNITY
PRAYER
ACCEPT
GOD
CHRIST
PLAN

BLAMELESS   EVANGELISE   WORSHIP
DANCING   FELLOWSHIP   OUTREACH
MINISTER   FORGIVE

   Published by The Open Bible Trust

Young Searchers

By Andrew and Andrea Marple

Worship

We often hear the word "worship" used on a Sunday morning at church: "Welcome to this morning's worship…" or, "Let's begin our worship with hymn number 73". Can you write down what you think of as worship?

_____

_____

Find Revelation chapter 4 and verse 11 to help you fill in the missing words:
"You are _____, our Lord and God, to receive _____ and _____ and _____, for you _____ all things."

So, worship begins with **recognising** God's worth and value

In the Old Testament, the Israelites worshipped God in lots of different ceremonies. Their worship involved them using all of their senses: sight, hearing, touch, smell and taste. Can you join the worship to the sense?

Many different instruments were used to make music and lots of songs can be found in the Bible.

Sacrifices were burnt and from them came a pleasant aroma.

Feasts were held to celebrate and remember special occasions. Much of the food was symbolic.

The tabernacle was full of beauty, with all the shades of colour having a symbolic meaning.

At the sacrifice, the people touched the head of the animal, showing that it was going to die in their place.

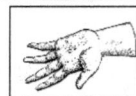

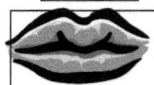

Look back at your answer to our first question. Most people would think of worship as singing, praising, praying, and maybe dancing in a church service. These are good answers and show that we value God and are responding to Him with thankfulness and praise. Can you find the following words connected with worship, hidden in this word search?

h	e	l	b	m	u	h	s	n	o	n	g
c	n	d	p	c	w	e	r	w	l	l	e
r	e	y	a	r	p	u	y	o	o	r	t
u	w	e	y	n	o	s	t	r	a	e	h
h	o	b	e	n	c	e	y	t	o	c	a
c	h	o	o	t	r	e	e	h	a	i	n
p	i	h	s	r	o	w	c	y	d	v	k
r	e	s	e	u	l	a	v	n	e	r	f
a	w	p	o	w	e	r	i	n	d	e	u
i	n	s	t	r	u	m	e	n	t	s	l
s	g	n	o	s	o	g	n	s	o	i	p
e	w	e	t	c	e	p	s	e	r	p	r

worship   instruments
heart   service
mind   obey
prayer   glory
songs   honour
dance   power
praise   humble
thankful   awe
worthy   value
respect   church

Worship that is pleasing to God involves our hearts, minds and wills in obedient service to Him. That means that our worship is more than what happens at church once a week. We are worshipping God whenever we do or say something that shows the value and respect with which we hold Him. In other words, the way we live our lives is an act of worship. Let us pray that God will help us to truly worship him:

> **Dear Lord, You are the one true God, Creator of the world and our Father in heaven. I thank you that I can worship you freely. Help me to worship you in what I say and do every day.**
>
> **I pray this in Christ's name. Amen.**

Young Searchers

By Andrew and Andrea Marple

Faith

Throughout the New Testament we find the word "faith" used many times. Faith is something very important in the life of every follower of the Lord Jesus Christ. So, let's discover what this word faith means, how we get it, and why it is so important.

What is faith?
One chapter in the Bible tells us a lot about "faith" and "faithful" people. It is Hebrews chapter 11. Can you find this chapter and read verse 1? For a Christian, having faith is having confidence and certainty of God's existence, and believing in His promises. In other words, being sure that God is real today and believing what we learn about Him.

Each of the following nine verses from Hebrews chapter 11 tells us about someone who had faith: verses 4, 5, 7, 8, 20, 21, 22, 24 and 31. Once you have the names, try to fit them into the grid below:

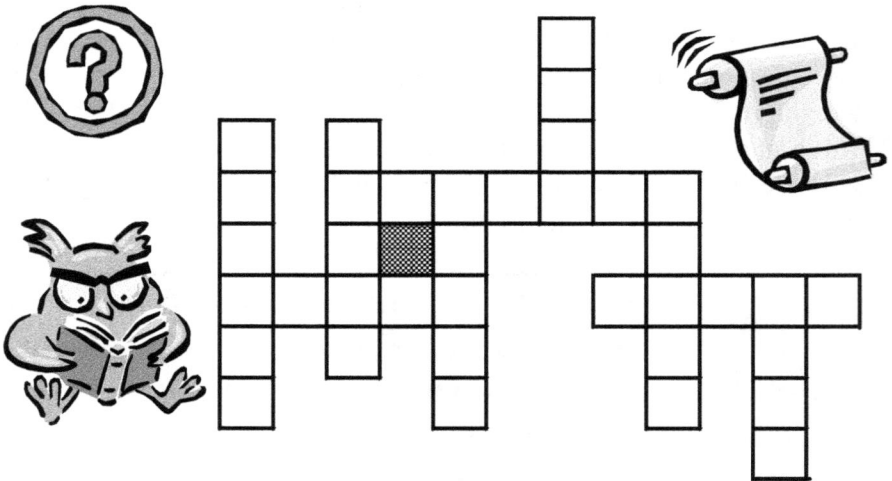

How do we get faith?

Read Romans chapter 10, verse 17 for an answer to this question. Faith comes from what we *learn* about God in the Bible. The more we learn about someone – what he has done for others (for example our local doctor or policeman) – the more we are able to have trust and faith in them and what they can do for us. So it is with God. Our faith in Him comes as we learn from other people about His character and love. We need to keep learning more about God so that our faith in Him can grow. Colour in this example of big faith!

Why is faith so important?

Our faith (or *belief*) that Jesus died on the cross for our sins is the whole basis of why we are Christians. Our sins have been forgiven and we have been saved from death to have eternal life with our gracious Heavenly Father. Read Ephesians chapter 2, verse 8.

We are told more in Hebrews chapter 11, verse 6. Find this passage so that you can fill in the missing words:

"And without _____ it is impossible to _____ God, because anyone who comes to him must _____ that he _____and that he rewards those who earnestly _____ him."

O Lord, our faith in You is such an important part of our life as a Christian. We thank You that we have teachers to help us learn more about You. We pray that as we learn, and our faith increases, we will love You more and be able to share Your love with others. We pray this in Christ's name. Amen.

Young Searchers

By Andrew and Andrea Marple

Shepherds and their Sheep

When we imagine as children which job we'd like when we grow up, being a shepherd probably isn't in our top ten! Maybe there's not a big demand for shepherds where you live, and even if there is, it doesn't sound particularly important or impressive does it?

In Biblical times, being a shepherd was a very demanding and important job. One famous shepherd in the Bible was Moses. After murdering an Egyptian, Moses ran away in to the land of Midian, and became a shepherd. Alone in the wilderness, he fed and cared for the sheep. He was learning about being responsible and brave. These were the skills he would need later in his life when God used him to become a great leader.

David was one of the greatest men in the Old Testament. He was many things - a musician, poet, soldier, king - but first of all he was a shepherd known for his skills and bravery. Remember when he killed Goliath the giant? He used the very sling normally used for firing at wild animals preying on his flock.

So why was looking after sheep so important? Having sheep in Biblical times was a sign of wealth. Sheep were very valuable creatures, used for food, clothing, tent materials and sacrifices. They could also be traded for other goods and services. But it was no easy task to look after these animals. They needed constant care and attention. For example, they quickly needed shelter if it rained, or else their wet wool would become so heavy that they would fall over and would be unable to get up again! Their feet were prone to foot rot, or they would wander away. And don't forget the hungry predators lurking nearby. Sheep really needed to be looked after….in fact a lot like people do!

In the Old Testament, God's people the Israelites were described as His flock. Read Ezekiel Ch.34, v.1-10 to see whether or not the religious leaders were doing a good job of looking after, or shepherding them. No, the Israelite sheep were in the hands of bad shepherds who were only feeding themselves and worrying about their own health. The sheep were abandoned and were scattering.

God reassured the Israelites that they would be properly cared for. Ezekiel Ch.34, v.31 says:
"You my sheep, the sheep of my pasture, are people, and I am your God, declares the Sovereign LORD."

In the New Testament of the Bible, God provides a perfect shepherd for His flock of believers – Jesus Christ. In what ways is Jesus a loving guide for His people? Find John Ch.10,
v.11: "I am the _____ _____. The _____ _____ lays down _____ _____ for the sheep."

v.14: "I am the _____ _____; I _____ ___ _____ and my sheep _____ ___."
____
v.16: "They too will listen to my voice, and there shall be _____ _____ and _____ _____."

Jesus cares for us. He is concerned about the weak and sick, and searches for the lost. He rules with love - gathering and protecting us. Psalm 23 v.1 says: "The LORD is my shepherd, I shall not be in want." If we obey the Lord and follow His guidance, we know that eternal life and security are ours.

Thank you Lord that You are our caring shepherd. Help us to use Your example each day to care for the weak, the lost, and the hungry.
In Christ's name we pray, Amen.

                              Published by The Open Bible Trust

Young Searchers

By Andrew and Andrea Marple

Forgiving

When someone says something hurtful or we feel we've been wronged, we naturally feel upset and angry. We dwell on what's happened and it can be a difficult step to take to forgive that person. It is the right step to take, however.

One amazing story of forgiveness is found at the beginning of the Bible. It is the story of Joseph. Read Genesis chapter 37 to see how Joseph was treated. We're told that Joseph had eleven older brothers who became very jealous of him, especially when their father Jacob made Joseph "a richly ornamented robe" – chapter 37, verse 3. They caught Joseph, sold him as a slave and then deceived their father into believing he had died.

So what happens to this family? Read Genesis chapters 39 to 50, which tell us the whole story. Joseph came face to face with his brothers again and, although he had been treated very badly, ultimately (chapter 50, verse 17) **Joseph forgave**.

Exodus chapter 1, verses 1-4 give you the names of all the brothers who were reunited in Egypt. Can you fit them into this puzzle?

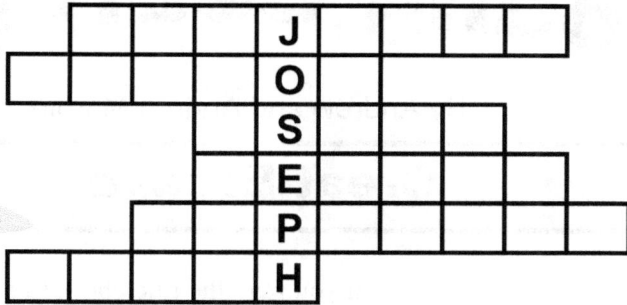

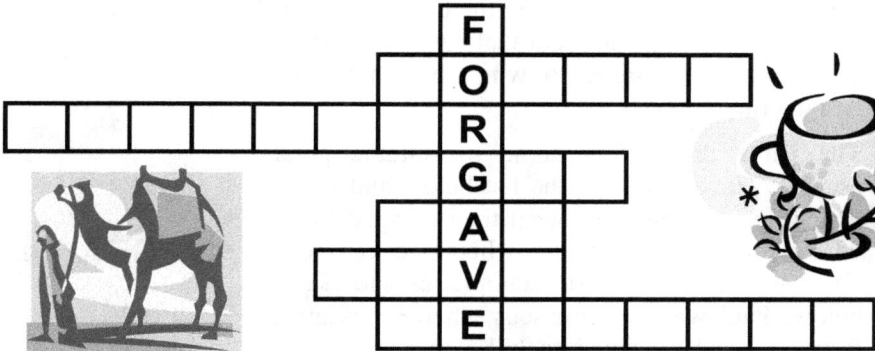

Peter is wondering about the act of forgiveness in Matthew chapter 18. See how Jesus answers his questions in verses 21-22:

"Lord, how many times shall I forgive my brother when he sins against me? Up to seven times?" Jesus answered, "I tell you, not seven times, but seventy-seven times." (Margin – "seventy times seven").

Jesus wants His disciples to have a spirit of endless forgiveness. Why might that be? Read what Jesus says next to Peter to illustrate this point (chapter 18, verses 23-35): **We are to forgive each other, just as our Heavenly Father has forgiven us.**

> **Dear Lord, thank you for the gift of Your Son, Jesus Christ, whose death on the cross forgave us our sins. Help us to turn away from doing wrong and to show more forgiveness for one another.**
> **We ask this in Christ's name, Amen.**

Young Searchers

By Andrew and Andrea Marple

Great Escapes

What do you think of when you read the title above? Perhaps you think of an escapologist such as Houdini; or an advert in a magazine trying to get you to spend a weekend in the countryside; or your favourite football team that came back from 0-3 down at half-time to win the Champions' League final.

The Bible tells us of some memorable great escapes. Have a look at the list below and try to match up: who escaped, what they escaped from, where this took place and where we can read about it in the Bible. For example, as underlined below, Paul was in Damascus when he escaped from Jews who wanted to kill him and we can read about this in Acts 9:23-25.

Who?	Where?	From What?	Bible Passage
Moses	**Damascus**	Prison	Exodus 12:31-40
Paul	Gaza	Jews searching for them	Acts 12:5-10
Israel	Jerusalem	**Jews who wanted to kill him**	Daniel 6:16-23
Spies	Egypt	Prison	Joshua 2:1-16
Samson	Philippi	Slavery	Exodus 2:11-15
Peter	Jericho	Lion's Den	Judges 16:1-3
Paul and Silas	Babylon	Punishment for killing an Egyptian	**Acts 9:23-25**
Daniel	Egypt	The Philistines	Acts 16:22-34

All of these great escapes were done through the power of God to ensure that His plans were continued. In the example given, Paul is lowered down the city walls of Damascus in a basket to escape. Read Acts 9:1-31. It tells us how Paul had been converted from persecuting Christians wherever he could find them, to becoming a Christian himself and immediately starting to preach about Jesus, the Son of God.

God had a tremendous plan for Paul, which would see him writing almost half the books of the New Testament and embarking on missionary journeys that would spread Christianity far and wide. Indeed, it can be claimed that Paul's conversion and life are the most important in human history after the life of Jesus Christ himself. All of this was in danger before Paul had even been able to leave Damascus. So God protected Paul, enabled him to escape and allowed him to carry out the wonderful ministry work that He had planned for him.

As you read through Acts 9:1-31 you will note that God used two people to help Paul to start this new phase in his life. The first was **Ananias**, whom God sent to Paul in Damascus to restore his eyesight and to fill him with the Holy Spirit. The second was **Barnabas**, who introduced Paul to the disciples in Jerusalem and persuaded them that he was now a Christian himself and that they need no longer fear him.

Just as Ananias and Barnabas supported Paul in his early Christian life, we should be ready to help and support new Christians ourselves, within the family of the church.

> **Dear Lord,**
>
> **We know that you have great plans for each and every one of us. Give us the courage and dedication to carry them out, as we know for sure that you will do everything in your power to help and support us.**
>
> **In Christ's name we pray, Amen.**

Young Searchers

By Andrew and Andrea Marple

Bull's-Eye

There are a number of definitions of '*sin*' in the Bible. If we look in the Old Testament, we see that the word 'sin' itself meant to fall short or to miss the target. One example of this is from Judges 20:16, which tells us about the Benjamite army:

"Among all these soldiers there were seven hundred chosen men who were left-handed, each of whom could sling a stone at a hair and not **miss**."

The sling was a very successful weapon in Old Testament times; a stone weighing about one pound could be thrown at speeds of up to 100 miles per hour! David demonstrated how effective the sling could be when he fought Goliath.

Another example of the word 'sin' from the Old Testament can be found in Daniel 9:4-5:

"O Lord, the great and awesome God, who keeps his covenant of love with all who love him and obey his commands, we have **sinned** and done wrong. We have been wicked and have rebelled; we have turned away from your commands and laws. "

Here the Jews had turned away from how God had told them to live their lives; they sinned, they missed the target that God had set for them.

But what is the meaning of 'sin' for us today, in the New Testament? Let's read from Romans 3:23-24:

"for all have **sinned** and fall short of the glory of God, and are justified freely by his grace through the redemption that came by Christ Jesus."

We have all sinned and fallen short of God's standards and the target he has set us. Just as Galatians 5:22-23 tells us that love, joy, peace, patience, kindness, goodness, faithfulness, gentleness and self-control come from God; the reverse is our sinful side of hate, conflict, impatience, cruelty, wickedness, disloyalty, violence and disobedience.

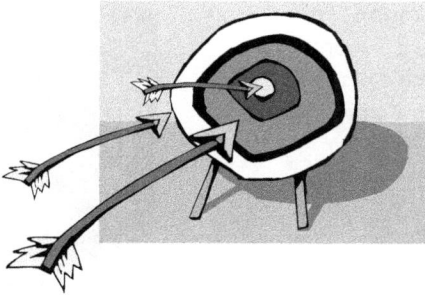

Sin is an important subject to address. It separates us from God, who is completely holy and without sin. The main reason that Jesus Christ came into the world was to deal with the problem of sin. We know now that our sins have been forgiven when Christ died for us on the cross.

In our daily lives we must try not to miss the target and fall short. Like a good archer, we should always be trying to hit the gold or bull's-eye in the very centre of the target. We have help to do this: Jesus Christ is the referee and judge; the disciples are our coaches; and the Bible is our rulebook and coaching manual.

Dear Lord,

Please help us each and every day to do our very best to meet the standards that you have set for us. Guide our aim towards love, patience and self-control in our lives.

In Christ's name we pray, Amen.

Young Searchers

By Andrew and Andrea Marple

God is calling you!

The first successful telephone was invented by Alexander Graham Bell on 10 March, 1876 and the first telephone call was: 'Come here, Mr Watson, I want you!'.

It wasn't until the 1960s that push button phones replaced dial phones and the first mobile phones didn't appear until the 1980s. Now it seems that everyone from the age of ten has their own mobile phone. How Alexander Graham Bell would marvel at the technology of today.

God Calls Samuel

In the Old Testament in 1 Samuel chapter 3, we read about God's call for Samuel. Read verses 1 – 10 and then answer the following questions:

5. Who did Samuel work under at the temple?

6. How many times did God call Samuel?

7. Who did Samuel think was calling him at first?

8. What did Samuel reply when God called him the first time?

9. What two objects within the temple does verse 3 tell us about?

Jesus Calls His First Disciples

Moving to the New Testament, Matthew chapter 4:18-22 tells us how Jesus Christ called His first disciples: Peter, Andrew, James and John. Read this passage and then answer the following questions:

1. Which lake was Jesus walking beside?

2. What do you think "fishers of men" means?

3. How long did Peter and Andrew and James and John take to think before they gave up their jobs and followed Jesus?

4. Who was Zebedee?

God is Calling You

A call from God is an invitation to follow Him and do His work here on Earth. God calls us all to something different, depending on our gifts and talents.

The telephone is always ringing. All we need to do is pick it up and answer God's call.

Word Search

Complete the following word search for the twelve disciples that Jesus initially called:

Z	S	E	M	A	J	P	E	T	R	E	A	M	Q
O	M	I	A	M	U	E	M	A	J	A	M	E	U
W	I	M	T	A	D	E	U	O	S	U	E	S	O
E	S	W	T	T	O	V	H	A	J	I	D	P	T
R	I	U	H	A	S	I	M	O	N	M	I	A	J
D	M	E	E	T	I	O	S	D	A	L	M	G	S
N	S	E	W	A	H	T	R	A	I	A	J	O	I
A	E	E	W	T	D	E	U	H	S	J	O	H	N
N	M	S	E	S	A	D	P	T	O	O	H	N	O
A	A	P	E	T	E	R	A	M	A	R	K	A	M
D	J	W	E	M	O	L	O	H	T	R	A	B	U
Q	U	L	I	H	P	I	L	I	T	Y	P	H	Z

BARTHOLOMEW
ANDREW
THADDAEUS
JAMES
SIMON
PHILIP
THOMAS
MATTHEW
JOHN
JAMES
JUDAS
PETER

We ask You Lord to help us answer Your call to us. Guide and show us how we might best use the gifts and talents You have given us to do Your will on Earth. Help us too to encourage others to answer Your call. In Christ's name we pray. Amen.

Young Searchers

By Andrew and Andrea Marple

The Vine and the Branches

During our recent travels we have enjoyed visiting a number of vineyards both in France and Canada. We have come to appreciate all the special care and specific conditions and procedures needed in order to have a fruitful and prosperous harvest. The whole process is now very technically advanced and commercially based, but the care of a vineyard in order to produce fruit has been well understood since Biblical times.

In John 15:1-8, Jesus wants us to recognise Him as "the true Vine". His followers are the branches connected to this vine by their living union with Christ. The intention is that Christians will feed and be nurtured from the central vine and produce much fruit: good works and a life lived according to God's purpose for us.

The grapevine can be very prolific, with a single vine bearing many grapes. In Psalm 80:8-9 grapes were a symbol of Israel's fruitfulness in doing God's work on Earth: "You brought a vine out of Egypt; you drove out the nations and planted it. You cleared the ground for it and it took root and filled the land."

Prepare to be Pruned

In this passage from John's gospel, God ("my Father") is "the Gardener". We can imagine the gardener caring for the branches in order to make them fruitful. He cares for us by pruning us in two different ways. John 15:2 says that branches that don't bear fruit are cut off. They are separated at the trunk because they have proved to be worthless – believers who haven't produced any fruit for God. The second kind of pruning is also

described in John 15:2. Branches that do bear fruit are cut back so that they will be even more fruitful.

So what does this mean in our lives? It means that when we are living our everyday lives close to Jesus Christ, we can still expect to have our characters and faith tested and ultimately strengthened from an experience of having been "cut back". Things will be ticking away nicely and we'll be in a comfortable routine in our home and church life, when we'll get some unexpected news about our health, job, or circumstances. We will need in these times to rely all the more on the nourishment and life offered by Christ, the vine.

Producing Fruit

Jesus says in John 15:5 "I am the vine; you are the branches. If a man remains in me and I in him, he will bear much fruit; apart from me you can do nothing." Apart from Christ our efforts are unfruitful. The only way to live a truly good life is to stay close and attached to Him. Verse 8 goes on to say "This is to my Father's glory". This is surely the whole purpose of our lives – to produce a harvest that honours the Harvester.

Now try and complete the word search below, using the list of words from John 15:1-8:

F	R	U	I	V	W	S	R	E	H	T	I	W	V		VINE
L	U	F	T	I	U	R	F	G	A	R	E	T	S		BRANCHES
E	L	V	T	N	F	E	F	R	I	U	T	U	G		GARDENER
P	T	H	R	E	R	A	V	I	U	E	F	A	R		FRUIT
G	E	R	P	R	U	N	E	S	E	T	R	R	E		PRUNES
A	S	R	R	R	I	E	E	H	I	D	U	F	I		FRUITFUL
R	T	V	I	N	K	H	N	R	E	R	I	F	N		BEAR
B	U	N	R	E	C	G	E	N	B	R	T	R	S		BURNED
E	C	U	T	N	F	I	E	R	I	E	B	U	F		CUTS
N	I	V	A	U	U	R	P	F	B	E	A	R	N		WITHERS
S	E	R	A	R	B	C	A	R	E	B	E	A	G		TRUE
A	B	U	R	N	E	D	R	U	A	V	I	E	R		FIRE

Young Searchers

By Andrew and Andrea Marple

Who do *you* say that He is?

In the Gospel of Matthew 16:13-16 Jesus asks some very important questions. Please read this passage.

After He had withdrawn from Galilee itself, Jesus continued preaching to the Jewish people further afield: firstly to the eastern shore of the Sea of Galilee, then to Phoenicia and the Decapolis, and finally to Caesarea Philippi, near the slopes of Mount Hermon. It is here that Jesus gathers His disciples together and asks them the following question:

"Who do people say the Son of Man is?"

If Jesus had been alive today, He would have asked His disciples what the word on the street was. What are the podcasts and blogs saying about me? What discussions are people having in web forums and Facebook groups? The disciples didn't have the benefit of access to today's sources of information. Instead they had to answer based on their face-to-face discussions with the Jewish people. The disciples gave Jesus the following answers to His question:

John the Baptist

John the Baptist had a reputation as someone new and fresh. He might have looked a bit weird but he was a fearless preacher, uncompromising in his message of repentance and announcing the arrival of Jesus Christ.

Try and find out some more about John the Baptist – he is mentioned in all four Gospels; his coming was predicted in the Old Testament and he is referred to again in the book of Acts.

Elijah

Elijah was Israel's most famous prophet. He was someone from the past who was dedicated and committed to God and through whom God accomplished many miracles.

We can learn more about Elijah by reading his story in 1 Kings 17:1 to 2 Kings 2:11.

Jeremiah

Jeremiah was a faithful messenger of God. He was emotional and compassionate, dedicated to justice. He had to depend on God's love as he developed his endurance.

Go to the book of Jeremiah to find out about the life of Jeremiah.

Each of these three great Biblical figures shares qualities and traits with Jesus Christ, but none is the correct answer. Then Jesus asks the same question to the disciples themselves. Peter immediately responds as follows:

"You are the Christ, the Son of the living God"

But who do *you* say that He is? Is He just a part of your family's life, a part of your family history? Is he just the icing on the cake of an already full and exciting life? Or is He truly the most important thing in your life, Jesus Christ, the Son of the living God and your Lord and Saviour?

To end with, try and link up the characters with facts from their lives:

John the Baptist ➡	Lived in the time of Ahab
	Father was Zacharias
	Lived in Anathoth
Elijah ➡	Lived in the time of king Herod
	Father was Hilkiah
Jeremiah ➡	Lived in Gilead

Young Searchers

By Andrew and Andrea Marple

Wealth

There's no denying that money plays an important part in our lives. Almost everyone needs to have money for food, shelter and clothing. So, is there anything wrong in having money? Well, the Bible doesn't condemn having money as such, but it does have a lot to say about our attitude towards money- how we think of it, how we get it, and what we do with it.

The dangers of money. Most people believe that the more money we have, the happier we'll be. In our desperation to get greater riches, we can fall into many traps, such as dishonesty and stealing. When Moses was receiving the laws for the Israelites, God told them not to cheat each other by using dishonest standards to measure and weigh (read Leviticus Ch.19, vs.35-36). Now read the story of Zacchaeus the tax collector in Luke Ch.19, vs. 1-10. From what Zacchaeus says in verse 18, how do you think he had become rich?

In the parable of the rich fool, the man produces a good crop, and this gives him a sense of security. He decides to hoard his grain and trusts in his wealth to take care of him for "many years" (Luke Ch.12, vs.15). Unfortunately, the man died, and is a "fool" because he stored up earthly riches but wasn't "rich towards God". Proverbs Ch.12, verse 28 tells us that "whoever trusts in his riches will fall".

The possession of money can also make people proud and boastful. Read about the only thing the Lord wants us to boast about in Jeremiah Ch.9, vs. 23-24.

In Hebrews Ch. 13, verse 5, there is a warning given: "Keep your lives free from the love of money…" Can you crack the following code to work out why?

	A	B	C	D	E
1	the	kinds	from	pierced	is
2	root	have	money	a	griefs
3	some	wandered	faith	themselves	of
4	eager	all	people	many	for
5	love	and	with	evil	but

E4　A1　A5　E3　C2　E1　D2　A2　E3　B4　B1　E3

D5　.　A3　C4　,　A4　E4　C2　,　B2　B3　C1

A1　C3　B5　D1　D3　C5　D4　E2　.

The right way to handle money. So, what should our attitude towards money be, and how can we keep from loving it? The Apostle Paul gives us some help in 1 Timothy Ch.6. Turn to this very important chapter. We are to realise that one day our riches here will all be gone (vs. 7 and 17). Verse 8 tells us to be content with what we have. We're to be careful of what we're willing to do to get more money. We are to trust God, and love doing good to others more than riches (verse 11). And importantly, anyone who has been blessed with money is to use it to do "good works" giving "happily to those in need always being ready to share with others what God has given them"(verse 18).

True wealth. As Christians, true wealth does not consist of what we own. Whatever we may or may not have in this world, we know we have everything in God, who is Lord of all. We have been enriched with the power to speak and know about God (1 Corinthians Ch.1, vs. 4-5). We have been shown the "incomparable riches of God's grace" (Ephesians Ch.2, verse7) when He sent His son Jesus Christ to die for our sins.

Paul assures us that "..my God will meet all your needs according to his glorious riches in Christ Jesus."(Philippians Ch.4, verse 19).

Dear Lord, Thank you for your many blessings to us. Help us in our attitude towards money so that we use your gifts to us wisely; remembering to share and help those in need. Teach us about the riches we have in you, so that our love for you radiates from us.

In Christ's name we pray, Amen.

Young Searchers

By Andrew and Andrea Marple

Conform or Transform

The book of Romans was written by the apostle Paul to the people of the church of Rome. The congregation there would have been made up of both Gentile and Jewish Christians. A study of the book of Romans is highly recommended. Paul clearly outlines the fundamentals of the Christian faith in the first eleven chapters and then we have the word "therefore" at the start of Romans 12. Paul now goes on to give practical guidance on how we should live our lives as Christians. He sets out the radical changes in thinking and behaviour that God expects of those who have put their faith in Jesus Christ as Saviour and Lord.

In this article, we want to concentrate on just two verses from this magnificent letter – Romans 12:1-2:

Living Sacrifices

"Therefore, I urge you, brothers, in view of God's mercy, to offer your bodies as living sacrifices, holy and pleasing to God—this is your spiritual act of worship. Do not conform any longer to the pattern of this world, but be transformed by the renewing of your mind. Then you will be able to test and approve what God's will is—his good, pleasing and perfect will."

Paul presents his readers with two distinct options:

1. **Conformation** to the way of the world, ignoring God's plan for us.

2. **Transformation** of our lives, allowing God to guide every aspect of the way we live.

Jesus Christ made the ultimate sacrifice on the cross for us – dying to save us from sin and death. As Christians, in return for all that Christ has done for us, it is really very little to ask to live our lives in a way that pleases him.

In all aspects of our lives we have the choice between conforming or transforming. In the home, at school, at work, when out and about with family and friends we can conform to the ways of the world with behaviour that is selfish, unkind, arrogant, uncaring and destructive. Or, we can be transformed, looking to Christ for the way we live with kindness, understanding, forgiveness and generosity.

So how can we be transformed? Paul tells us that it is by the renewing of our minds. If we can start to transform our thoughts then our actions will follow. Try and transform the following jumbled letters from the remainder of Romans 12 into words:

egcra		**luffatih**	
gecuorane		**cryme**	
ovle		**jeoreic**	
eepac		**ecrines**	
lufhcreeyl		**yamhonr**	

When people see us living our lives is it obvious that we are Christians? Does our behaviour set us apart? Or can we not be distinguished from the world around us: swearing, cursing and behaving just like everyone else. Being a Christian is the greatest gift but it also comes with great responsibilities. We must let our salvation transform everything we do and allow God to guide every aspect of our lives.

Dear Lord,
Help us to transform our minds step by step and in doing so transform our lives for You. May our lives be examples to those around us of our faith in You.
In Christ's name we pray, Amen.

Three Gifts

T	Y	R	A	S	R	E	V	I	N	N	A
R	O	T	E	R	T	I	A	R	Y	W	T
S	A	M	T	S	I	R	H	C	A	E	R
I	T	R	E	B	L	E	T	O	D	D	Y
R	T	N	E	L	A	T	P	R	H	D	T
O	F	F	E	R	I	N	G	S	T	I	I
O	W	B	E	S	T	O	W	E	R	N	L
R	E	W	O	P	E	S	T	F	I	G	I
E	T	E	R	N	A	R	Y	H	B	O	B
F	O	G	I	V	E	L	P	I	R	T	A
F	G	S	A	C	R	I	F	I	C	E	S
O	F	E	E	A	P	T	I	T	U	D	E

THREE
TRIPLE
TREBLE
GIFTS
ABILITY
TALENT
POWER
GIVE
BESTOW
OFFER
TERTIARY

APTITUDE   TERNARY   OFFERINGS
PRESENTS   SACRIFICES   ANNIVERSARY
WEDDING   BIRTHDAY   CHRISTMAS

    Published by The Open Bible Trust

Young Searchers

By Andrew and Andrea Marple

Three Essential Gifts for those who are Searching – Part 1

How can **we** as young searchers feel a sense of optimism and confidence about the future? We might dream of affluence, continued improvements in medical research and communications and have ambitions. But with all life's uncertainties and the events on the news, we can't rely on these things to give our lives direction. For real confidence and optimism we need to have a strong sense of **identity**, **belonging** and **purpose**. Unfortunately society is often failing to provide any of these; but we can rely on God.

The Bible shows us that through Jesus Christ, God has offered us a **new identity**, **a new destiny**, and **a new purpose in living**. As well as being gifts from God, these three things are also ideals to strive for, and virtues to learn. Today we'll consider the first gift:

Gift #1 – A Sense of Identity

As travelling expatriates, our family is often asked to produce various pieces of identification: at different airports, for immigration officials, new employment, school and medical purposes. They show who we are, where we're from, and admit us to where we want to go. Outwardly we can be identified and recognised; yet who are we really, and where is our place of belonging? A lack of identity and sense of belonging can be a major problem besetting young and older people alike. What's the answer?

Become a Child of God

"Yet to all who receive him (Jesus Christ), to those who believed in his name, he gave the right to become **children of God**." John 1:12.

"How great is the love the Father has lavished on us, that we should be called **children of God**. And that is what we are! The reason the world does not know us is that it did not know him." 1 John 3:1.

Christ is God's Son by nature, while *our* sin separates us from him (Romans 3:23). By becoming a Christian, our faith justifies us and by God's grace we are allowed to become God's adopted sons. Adoption is mentioned five times in the New Testament. It was common among the Greeks and Romans who granted the adopted son all the privileges of a natural son. Ephesians 1:5 says: (In love)...he predestined us to be adopted as his sons through Jesus Christ in accordance with his pleasure and will." It was his plan for us before our actual birth. **This is our identity!**

Being a Child of God

The Bible tells us that we gain other new relationships by being adopted by God. Read Mark 3:31-35. Our identity in God's spiritual family is more important than our identity in out human families. Read about our brotherhood with Jesus in Hebrews 2:10-12. In our adoption, we now have **God as our Father**. We have a close, loving relationship with him and can pray with boldness and assurance that he will answer our prayers.

As God's child we can expect discipline from him because he loves us and he wants to correct our faults, giving us encouragement and perseverance to develop as his children. Read Hebrews 12:4-11. In the next edition of Search we will look at the second gift – A Sense of Direction.

> **Thank You Lord that through faith in Jesus Christ I am your child. With a new identity I can feel a sense of security, belonging and love.**
> **In Christ's name we pray, Amen.**

Young Searchers

By Andrew and Andrea Marple

Three Essential Gifts for those who are Searching – Part 2

Last time we began thinking about how young searchers, or Christians, can feel a sense of optimism and confidence about the future. We defined our identity – who are we – and concluded that, by faith in Jesus Christ, God forgives us our sins, accepts us as we are, and adopts us as His children. God is our father and we have a new identity. God then offers us a second gift:

Gift #2 – A Sense of Direction

What is it we want to feel optimistic about? Is it that we'll have the love of family and friends? Or we'll have the material things (job, money, possessions, etc.) we feel we need for a happy life? Optimism isn't always easy, but it is a healthy mental emotion and a good measure of our potential success in life. One reason for optimism is knowing where we're heading and where we belong.

We are citizens of heaven

"… many live as enemies of the cross of Christ. Their destiny is destruction, their god is their stomach, and their glory is in their shame. Their mind is on earthly things. **But our citizenship is in heaven**. And we eagerly await a Saviour from there, the Lord Jesus Christ, who, by the power that enables him to bring everything under his control, will transform our lowly bodies so that they will be like his glorious body." Philippians 3:18-21.

We are described as 'citizens of heaven' because the risen Christ is in Heaven and we are united with Christ as God's sons. Although we live on this earth, the Bible tells us not to love the world of sin that surrounds us; read 1 John 2:15-17. We should be striving to think more about heavenly things and less about earthly things.

We are aliens in this world

Being a citizen of heaven means we are aliens, or foreigners, in this world. The Bible tells us that our lifestyle should have an effect on those who don't yet believe in Jesus Christ: read 1 Peter 2:9-12. We're told in verse 12 that unbelievers 'may see your good deeds and glorify God on the day he visits us'. The Greek word 'see' refers to a careful watching over a period of time. We should be learning about what makes a good deed and a good life so that we can maybe influence the unbeliever to repent and believe. Read Hebrews 11:13-16 to find out where Abraham and Sarah were destined for.

We are heirs of hope

Which future event causes a Christian to be optimistic, or hopeful, about their future? Philippians 3:20 says "But our citizenship is in heaven. And we eagerly await a Saviour from there, the Lord Jesus Christ..." Christ <u>will</u> come again, and God <u>will</u> complete the process of transforming us. Some people try and improve their 'lowly bodies' with cosmetic surgery, and all kinds of treatments. But because of sin, earthly bodies are still subject to weakness, decay and death. The transformation Jesus Christ brings

will be better and deeper. Furthermore we have 'the hope that is stored up for (you) in heaven' (Colossians 1:5). This 'hope' isn't wishful thinking but a firm assurance that eternal life is our destiny.

Thank You Lord that through hope in Jesus Christ, heaven is my home. We pray that the Holy Spirit will help us to see clearly where we need to grow. Help us to learn heavenly qualities and ways of thinking rather than worldly ones.

In Christ's name we pray, Amen.

Young Searchers

By Andrew and Andrea Marple

Three Essential Gifts for those who are Searching – Part 3

The Bible shows us that, through Jesus Christ, God offers us the Christian way of life. To help equip us with confidence for this new life, three essential gifts are ours to learn about and strive for. God offers us: **a new identity**, a new destiny, or **sense of direction**, and thirdly:

Gift #3 – A Sense of Purpose

One definition of "purpose" is "the reason for which anything is done, created or exists". It is important to have a purpose in life - to begin to understand why God made the earth and created us to live on it. What is the reason for our existence? What does God require of us and others who share this purpose?

God requires us to Love

Read the parable of the Good Samaritan in Luke 10:29-37. The three people who come across the Jewish victim are the priest, the Levite and the Samaritan. Because of the hostility between Jews and Samaritans, the Samaritan on his donkey was the least likely to show care and compassion to the injured man. Yet Jesus details all of his loving actions.

So what kind of "love" is Jesus commanding? The word is used very freely in our language today, usually to describe feelings and emotions. Our common misconceptions about what love is can make this subject seem soppy, or rude, or certainly embarrassing. Rather than feelings, however, Jesus requires practical love- love that is inclined to show itself by the actions of **children of God**. Furthermore, this love we are to have for

Visit www.obt.org.uk for more resources

God and others is not out of a feeling of compulsion or duty. We are truly able to love God and others as a result of us first experiencing God's love. 1 John 4:19 says "We love because He first loved us."

Read 1 John 4: 7-21. Verse 12 says "No-one has ever seen God; but if we love one another, God lives in us and his love is made complete in us." God is progressively making us into the people we should be.

Loving God is different from loving family, friends, strangers or enemies. 1 John 5:3 says "This is love for God: to obey his commands. And his commands are not burdensome..." we're told because the Holy Spirit enables believers to obey.

1 Corinthians 13:13 says" And now these three remain: faith, hope and love. But the greatest of these is love." God is love; He showed it to us by sending His Son to die for our sins and so **loving one another is our fulfilling purpose in life.**

In the first of these three studies we asked how **we** as young searchers could feel a sense of optimism and confidence about the future. We need to remember this summary of our identity, destiny and purpose:

God is my Father.

Heaven is my Home.

Love is my task.

Heavenly Father, we praise You for these truths. Help us when we have negative thoughts or anxiety-especially about the future- to replace them with this saying. We pray that these three gifts become a reality in our lives and the lives of others. Amen.

More for Young People

Introducing God's Word

This was written by three school teachers, who are also three Sunday School teachers: Carol Brown, Lynn Mrotek and Michael Penny. It is a companion book to *Introducing God's Plan* and takes the reader through the Bible from Genesis to Revelation with

- puzzles,
- word searchers,
- crosswords,
- anagrams, etc.

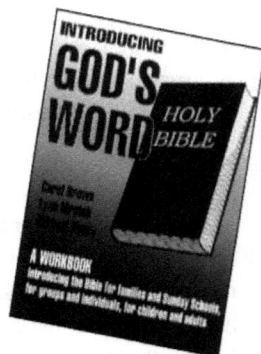

"There is a useful first page on introducing the Bible which includes Bible study helps, using many different methods to bring out the message. For example, when looking at the prophets there is (1) a word search, (2) fill the spaces, and (3) true or false questions. Other methods of questioning are crosswords, sentence gaps, jumbled words, group work and so on.

As I went through the book I found that there was much which could be used with profit for young and old alike. I liked the idea of giving an overview of the Bible to a generation that has little understanding of its message. It could be used by both church and school teachers needing 'something to edify and occupy'." **(Reviewed by Ken Blackwell in *Digest*, Association of Christian Teachers, UK)**

"With its clear format, it uses a variety of learning approaches and methods which should appeal to the inquisitive mind. It could also be used in a group setting such as a Sunday school.

This book incorporates the Old Testament and includes history books and prophets as well as a New Testament section which includes letters of Paul. **(Reviewed in *The War Cry* of the Salvation Army, UK)**

Copies be ordered from **www.obt.org.uk**

Introducing God's Plan

Sylvia and Michael Penny

The book is well presented with

- large easy-to-read print,
- punctuated with line drawings,
- maps and
- photos.

It consists of 16 chapters, eight on the Old Testament and eight on the New.

- After each chapter, there are three or four questions to answer.
- These are followed by a summary of God's plan up to that point, which builds up an overall view as readers progress.
- After that there are some puzzles, like a word search or spot-the-difference or anagrams, based on some aspect of the current chapter, and which reinforces what has been read.
- Finally there is a section giving the main Bible references used in that chapter.

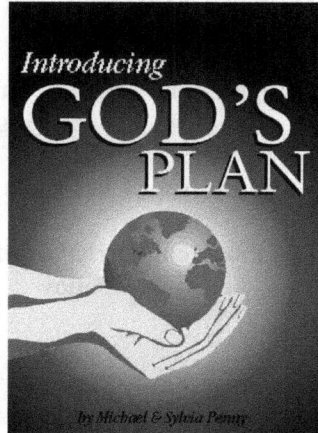

This is an ideal book, not only for private reading, but also for Religious Education in schools, children in Sunday Schools, and home groups for adults who have, perhaps, just completed something like the Alpha Course, or who have little knowledge of the Bible.

This book is a companion to *Introducing God's Word.*

**Further details of these books can be seen on www.obt.org.uk
They can be ordered from that website and also from
The Open Bible Trust, Fordland Mount,
Upper Basildon, Reading.**

**They are also available as eBooks from Amazon and Apple
And as KDP paperbacks from Amazon.**

The Balanced Christian Life

Michael Penny

A series of five studies based on Ephesians exploring

The Blessing Christians have in Christ
&
The Practical Christian life which should follow.

This is a large A4 size book. The right hand pages (which can be freely photocopied for groups) consist of questions and tasks for the individual to work through or for the group to work through and discuss.

Once they have done that, they can then look at the left hand page which gives suggested answers, comments and explanations.

This book, with its flexible style, is not only usefully for individual study, it is also ideal for:

- Lent groups,
- Post Alpha Groups,
- House Groups,
- Bible Study Groups.

An excellent, easy introduction
to Paul's greatest letter.

Further details of these books can be seen on www.obt.org.uk
They can be ordered from that website and also from
The Open Bible Trust, Fordland Mount,
Upper Basildon, Reading.

They are also available as eBooks from Amazon and Apple
And as KDP paperbacks from Amazon.